SPIRITUAL INTERVIEWS WITH
THE GUARDIAN SPIRIT OF
GEORGE LUCAS
AND THE SPIRIT OF
CARRIE FISHER

HS PRESS

RYUHO OKAWA

SPIRITUAL INTERVIEWS WITH THE GUARDIAN SPIRIT OF GEORGE LUCAS AND THE SPIRIT OF CARRIE FISHER

AWAKENING MESSAGES TO THE SPACE AGE

ALSO INCLUDES SPIRITUAL INTERVIEW WITH THE GUARDIAN SPIRIT OF LEONARDO DICAPRIO

HS PRESS

Copyright © 2021 by Ryuho Okawa
English translation © Happy Science 2021
Original title: *George Lucas Syugorei & Carrie Fisher no Reigen*
- Star Wars *ga Unagasu Uchu Jidai e no Mezame*-
HS Press is an imprint of IRH Press Co., Ltd.
Tokyo
ISBN 13: 978-1-943928-14-9
ISBN 10: 1-943928-14-2

Cover Image: AlexandrBognat/shutterstock.com

The opinions of the spirits do not necessarily reflect those of Happy Science Group.
For the mechanism behind spiritual messages, see the end section.

Contents

Preface 9

CHAPTER ONE

Spiritual Interview with Carrie Fisher

1 *Star Wars: Episode IX* and a Visiting Spirit 14

2 The Meaning of the Force 21

3 *Star Wars* and the God of the Universe 25

4 She Suggests Contact with Lucas' Guardian Spirit ... 32

CHAPTER TWO

Spiritual Interview with the Guardian Spirit of George Lucas

1 One of the American New Religious Teachings 40

2 Main Concept: The Pursuit of God's Force 42

3 *Star Wars* Is the Reality of the Universe 47

4 The Battle between the Light-Side and the Dark-Side ... 53

5 Who Is Lucas' Spiritual Teacher? 58

6 Influence from Kurosawa and Lucas' Past Lives 62

7 Promoting People's Awakening to the Space Age ... 66

8 I Might Be the "Pre-advice" of the Great Savior 71

9 What He Hopes for Future Space Movies 74

EXTRA CHAPTER

Spiritual Interview with the Guardian Spirit of Leonardo DiCaprio

1 Spiritual Secrets of Leonardo DiCaprio

   DiCaprio's guardian spirit frowns to a particular phrase ... 82

   Have the victims of Titanic gone up to heaven? 85

   Connection between DiCaprio's guardian spirit and
   God Odin 88

   If DiCaprio were to appear in a Happy Science movie ... 93

   How DiCaprio was able to win an Academy Award with
   the movie, *The Revenant* 97

   DiCaprio's G.S. and the Spirit World he belongs to 100

2 Becoming Famous Worldwide

   Movies and entertainment have the power to make you
   famous worldwide 104

   Through art and music, convey to people that the Great
   One was born 106

   "I want to give advice to your entertainment sections" ... 110

   Messages from DiCaprio's G.S. 114

Chapters One & Two were recorded in English.
Extra chapter was originally recorded in Japanese and later translated into English.

Afterword 119

About the Author 121
What Is El Cantare? 122
What Is a Spiritual Message? 124
About Happy Science 128
About Happiness Realization Party 132
Happy Science Academy Junior and Senior High School 133
Happy Science University 134
Contact Information 136
About IRH Press 138
Books by Ryuho Okawa 139
Music by Ryuho Okawa 153

Preface

I have compiled the spiritual messages from the guardian spirit of George Lucas, the father of the world famous *Star Wars*, and the late Carrie Fisher. This is a bitext in English and Japanese.*

This year Fall, Happy Science will be releasing the movie, *The Laws of the Universe Part 2—The Age of Elohim*, so as an introductory to understanding it, I wanted to ask about the concept of the Hollywood version of The Laws of the Universe. It appears the spirit of George Lucas is related to Zoroaster and the strong images of Light and Darkness and Jedi came down. The battle for Space Justice has been happening not only in the fictional world of movies but also in reality through the past, present, and future.

We also received a spiritual message of encouragement from the guardian spirit of Leonardo DiCaprio. I just pray that the messages we want to convey through The Laws of the Universe reach the world.

Ryuho Okawa
Master & CEO of Happy Science Group
Aug. 14, 2021

---

* This is about this book's original publication in Japan.

CHAPTER ONE

Spiritual Interview with Carrie Fisher

*Recorded January 7, 2020
in the Special Lecture Hall of Happy Science in Japan.*

In this chapter, the interviewer is symbolized as A.

Carrie Fisher (1956 - 2016)

An American actress and screenwriter. She became famous after starring as Princess Leia in the first *Star Wars* series in 1977. She again played the role as Princess Leia for the first time in almost 30 years in the 2015 movie, *Star Wars Episode VII: The Force Awakens*. Fisher passed away in 2016 due to a heart attack. Her last work was *Star Wars Episode VIII: The Last Jedi* (released December 2017), which had been shot few months prior. Fisher appeared in the 2019 movie, *Star Wars Episode IX: The Rise of Skywalker*, using deleted scenes from prequels in the series.

*Spiritual Interviews with the Guardian Spirit of
George Lucas and the Spirit of Carrie Fisher*

1

Star Wars: Episode IX and a Visiting Spirit

INTERVIEWER A
May I ask your name?

CARRIE FISHER
Ca...

A
Good evening. May I ask your name?

FISHER
Le... Princess Leia.

A
Eh? Oh, you were Princess Leia?

FISHER
Uh-huh.

A
The actress?

FISHER
Uh-huh.

A
You passed away.

FISHER
Uh-huh.

A
Can you speak Japanese?

FISHER
Uh-huh. Ah.

A
A little?

FISHER
I'll try. I'll try it. I'll try. I try, try. Thank you for coming (to the movie).

Spiritual Interviews with the Guardian Spirit of George Lucas and the Spirit of Carrie Fisher

A

Please wait a minute. [*Takes out the pamphlet of the movie*] Are you Ms. Carrie Fisher? Please look. See.

FISHER

Huh?

A

You?

FISHER

Sure. Sure. I am.

A

Do you understand your death?

FISHER

Huh?

A

Your death?

FISHER

Yeah. I'm dead.

A

Do you know Master Ryuho Okawa?

FISHER

Hmm… Fifty percent. About 50 percent, I know.

A

We watched *Star Wars* today.

FISHER

Yeah, I know.

A

So, you could come here.

FISHER

Uh, yeah. In some meaning, yes. In another meaning… yeah.

*Spiritual Interviews with the Guardian Spirit of
George Lucas and the Spirit of Carrie Fisher*

A
Why?

FISHER
You also have interest in *Star Wars*-like space story. You're making a new animation movie, *The Laws of the Universe*. Oh, yeah. And your conception from *Star Wars* Number 9...

A
Yes, Number 9.

FISHER
...is not so good? Not so good? You want to say so?

A
No, no. Hmm... a little.

FISHER
A little?

A
A little... I felt a lack of enlightenment.

FISHER
Enlightenment is very, very very difficult. Yeah, indeed! We made more than two hours' story, but enlightenment is only two or three minutes, maybe.

A
But we are religion people.

FISHER
Ah, religious people?

A
Ah, religious people. So... but... but you tried your best. For example, like Zen...

FISHER
Ah, you appreciated our movie?

A
Yes, yes. Good job.

Spiritual Interviews with the Guardian Spirit of
George Lucas and the Spirit of Carrie Fisher

FISHER

Thank you, thank you. I, indeed, am not the existence of this world, but I can appear on the screen, and it's very lucky for me and thankful to Mr. George Lucas. And I hope my job and our jobs are good influence on the people of the world, of course, people living in Japan, I hope so.

2

The Meaning of the Force

FISHER

Can you understand the meaning of *Jedi*? And the difference between light and darkness? It's a key point. It's very simple, but it's from the ancient age like the Mani sect or Zarathustra teaching from the Middle East. Light and evil. Yeah, it's very difficult to distinguish.

Even now, you are struggling regarding Hong Kong or Uyghur or China, yeah, and...

A

Iran.

FISHER

...Iran and America. It's very, very difficult which one you belong to. It's very difficult for the people to understand. Yeah, supreme commander, leader, is good or bad? It's very difficult. You are oriental people? You can understand oriental enlightenment or Zen-like thinking or yoga-like thinking, and of course, you know kendo. Yeah, and maybe concentration and the Force.

Spiritual Interviews with the Guardian Spirit of
George Lucas and the Spirit of Carrie Fisher

A

Princess Leia.

FISHER

Hai (in Japanese).

A

Princess Leia is a Jedi.

FISHER

Yeah.

A

One of the Jedi. And she is also a general.

FISHER

Yeah.

A

So, when you played the role of Princess Leia, what did you feel was important?

FISHER

What's important for me?

A

Yeah. What was important for you? You are also a Jedi.

FISHER

I wanted to keep "what is a good mind to be kept." Good will and good influence. Its name is legend. The people of this world now require a new legend to be good and to live with justice. If we can do something about that, it's my pleasure, I'm very happy.

And you want to contact George Lucas? Yeah, he is an ancient person, and also the universal person of the future. He, in some meaning, worked in the realm of God, I think.

A

In *Star Wars*, there was no God. But...

FISHER

Yeah. Jedi and...

*Spiritual Interviews with the Guardian Spirit of
George Lucas and the Spirit of Carrie Fisher*

A

The Force.

FISHER

...and the Sith or Darth Vader, that kind of dark-minded people are the replacement of devils.

A

What do you think is the Force?

FISHER

Yeah. It means men are not mortal and not trapped by body only. We are supreme beings and our real field is outside of the body. We can, I can, in some meaning, succeed in teaching people of the world about that.

You, religious people, also want to do that, but through the tool of movie—it's a very shallow teaching, I agree with that—it's a very shallow and very fundamental teaching, but I could, we could, yeah, make a success in this meaning. It means real leaders are spiritual beings, and also, the spiritual leaders sometimes separate good and evil, saint and evil. Yeah, it's a truth of the world.

3

Star Wars and the God of the Universe

A

Now, you are a spiritual being?

FISHER

Yes.

A

So, how do you feel as a spiritual being?

FISHER

Yeah. My job in this world has finished, and I must search for a new job in another world. But I, myself, want to do a space-related job in the spiritual world, if possible. There are many space people in reality, so I want to introduce them to you.

A

You believe in the existence of space people.

FISHER

No, no, no. I don't "believe." I just discovered or understood that. It's real. Yeah, real, *Star Wars* is real.

A

Have you met space people?

FISHER

Yes, of course.

A

For example?

FISHER

It's difficult, but there are, I don't know if it's Resistance or not, but the space people from the shadow space of the universe, and of course, the people from the light. So, the spiritual world is not limited to this Earth only. We have space people in the next world. And I'm planning to contact Mr. George Lucas' guardian spirit. He is one of the quite impressive and some kind of, how do you say, the disguised portion of God. I think so.

A
OK. Now, do you live in heaven?

FISHER
I hope so.

A
Yeah. OK. Do you believe in God?

FISHER
Yes, of course.

A
Your God's name, please tell me.

FISHER
God is God.

A
[*Laughs.*] The large print God?

FISHER
Yes. *The* God.

*Spiritual Interviews with the Guardian Spirit of
George Lucas and the Spirit of Carrie Fisher*

A
The God.

FISHER
No one can see Him. So, God is God. But the concept of *Star Wars* is not so misleading. It's a reality. It's coming soon and it's already coming. We are surrounded by such kind of space people in this earthly world, of course. Only Master Okawa understands that.

A
OK.

FISHER
If possible, we want to assist you in this field.

A
Oh, thank you very much. Do you know Natalie Portman?

FISHER
Yes.

Spiritual Interview with Carrie Fisher

A
She also played the role of Princess Amidala in *Star Wars*.

FISHER
Yes, yes, yes, yes.

A
And we have contacted her guardian spirit.

FISHER
Ah, really?

A
So, are you friends with her (guardian spirit) in heaven?

FISHER
Hmm...

A
No?

*Spiritual Interviews with the Guardian Spirit of
George Lucas and the Spirit of Carrie Fisher*

FISHER

She's very young and still living in this world. She is not dead, so our contact is very limited.

A

Hmm. Oh, right.

FISHER

I think she is a very good person and maybe she is a cutting-figure in this Hollywood world.

A

There is a meaning to the *Star Wars* movie.

FISHER

Yes, yes, yes.

A

It's not just a movie, you mean.

FISHER

Yes, yes, yes.

A
OK.

FISHER
It's a too long, long story, too dramatic, and has a lot of fiction in it. But if you say it has no spiritual meaning or God's Will, I want to say, "Oh, it has. We are thinking about that. This is the God of the Universe, one of his missions, we revealed." I think so.

Spiritual Interviews with the Guardian Spirit of George Lucas and the Spirit of Carrie Fisher

4

She Suggests Contact with Lucas' Guardian Spirit

FISHER

You are making a new animation video, *The Laws of the...*

A

...*Universe II* (*The Laws of the Universe-The Age of Elohim*, scheduled to be released in October 2021).

FISHER

...*Universe II* and *III*. It's very lucky even for Japanese people to understand the laws of the universe. You need the standpoint of the universal person, I think so.

A

Star Wars movie is made by inspiration from the universe?

FISHER

Yes, yes, yes, yes. Please check George Lucas' guardian spirit. He is almost the same grade spirit as Stan Lee, who left this world and came to this world, yeah. Almost the same mission, I think so.

A
Two years after your death, Stan Lee has gone. Have you met him?

FISHER
Yes.

A
Oh!

FISHER
I met him.

A
OK. So, we are looking forward to having a conversation (with George Lucas' guardian spirit).

FISHER
And I've heard Mr. Stan Lee, he's a dead man, but he is also a living man in this world, or another world, and he instructed you to make a new movie.

Spiritual Interviews with the Guardian Spirit of
George Lucas and the Spirit of Carrie Fisher

A
Yeah.

FISHER
So, it's very lucky for you.

A
Yeah.

FISHER
So, also, we George Lucas team making the *Star Wars* series want to assist you.

A
By the way, do you have a memory of your...

FISHER
[*Sighs deeply.*]

A
...space, another planet?

FISHER
Oh... Hmm...

A

I think you lived not only on Earth, but also on another planet.

FISHER

Hmm. Maybe it's far from this solar system. Ah, yeah, far from here. It's very, very far from here.

A

A different galaxy.

FISHER

Yeah. But I have much sympathy with the name "Pleiades." Maybe I have my origin in Pleiades.

A

OK. Thank you for coming today.

FISHER

Thank you. If possible, please contact George Lucas. I recommend it.

A

OK, thank you very much.

CHAPTER TWO

Spiritual Interview with the Guardian Spirit of George Lucas

Recorded January 8, 2020
in the Special Lecture Hall of Happy Science in Japan.

George Lucas (1944 - Present)

An American movie director, producer, and screenwriter. He is the creator of the *Star Wars* and *Indiana Jones* series, which were megahits around the world. Lucas studied film production at the University of Southern California and later established his own film company, Lucasfilm. He became famous after directing the 1973 movie, *American Graffiti*, which was successful. In 1977, Lucas worked on the first *Star Wars* series by himself, from directing to editing, because no one could understand his worldview. Due to the overwhelming amount of work and stress, he was hospitalized twice during the shooting, but the movie saw worldwide success, and it served to change people's view of sci-fi movies as a major genre. Lucas has received great influence from Akira Kurosawa and world's mythologies.

Interviewer from Happy Science

Sayaka Okawa[*]

> Vice Chairperson,
> Chief of CEO's Office,
> Religious Affairs Headquarters

The other two are symbolized as B and C.

---
[*] Her professional title represents her position at the time of the interview.

Spiritual Interviews with the Guardian Spirit of George Lucas and the Spirit of Carrie Fisher

1

One of the American New Religious Teachings

RYUHO OKAWA

Good morning, everyone. OK, we'd like to summon the guardian spirit of George Lucas. This is the first time for me. He's very famous for his films like the *Star Wars* series and the *Indiana Jones* series. Even Japanese people know him.

I guess the American new thinking and the teaching of the religious part come from, one is the *Avengers* series. This is the hero and anti-hero stories. It's a god or angel versus devils, demons. Another one is the George Lucas film, *Star Wars*. It's like the Hong Kong problem now, the gigantic empire versus small resistance stories. It's a huge, huge story, but in its story there is written what is light and what is darkness.

For example, how do you look at me (in these clothes)? Do I resemble Darth Vader or not? I don't know exactly, but for example, there appears "the Force," and the concept or recognition of the Force is very difficult even for the movie

Spiritual Interview with the Guardian Spirit of George Lucas

fans. But George Lucas maybe thinks that the oriental thinking regarding Zen or yoga-like Buddhism and the American-like justice, and his thinking is just around these two pillars. So, he himself suffered a lot because no one could understand what he is thinking about and wants to describe.

To tell the truth, I met the spirit of Princess Leia, the actress who played her, truly (See Chapter One). She has gone three years ago. In the midnight, she said, "Please interview the guardian spirit of George Lucas. You can find a new aspect." She said so, and so we want to contact him. OK then, I'll call him. Are you ready? OK.

Then, could I call the guardian spirit of Mr. George Lucas, famous movie director and producer? Mr. George Lucas' guardian spirit, would you come down here? [*About 20 seconds of silence.*]

*Spiritual Interviews with the Guardian Spirit of
George Lucas and the Spirit of Carrie Fisher*

2
Main Concept: The Pursuit of God's Force

GEORGE LUCAS' GUARDIAN SPIRIT
Umm.

INTERVIEWER B
Good morning.

LUCAS' G.S.
Ah, good morning.

B
Are you the guardian spirit of Mr. George Lucas?

LUCAS' G.S.
Yeah, of course.

B
Thank you very much for coming to Happy Science today. It's very honorable and we are a big fan of your *Star Wars*

series, so we are so happy to have an interview with you today. Thank you very much.

LUCAS' G.S.
He is still alive, so I am a representative of him. A little different. But I can almost understand what he is thinking, and of course, I have been giving him a lot of inspiration, so yeah, I can answer you.

B
Thank you very much. So, first of all, the last episode, *Episode IX*, was just released.

LUCAS' G.S.
Episode IX? The new one? Ah, yeah. OK.

B
It concludes the *Star Wars* series, and it's a great success not only in Japan but all over the world (at the time of recording).

Spiritual Interviews with the Guardian Spirit of
George Lucas and the Spirit of Carrie Fisher

LUCAS' G.S.

Thank you, thank you very much.

B

My first question to you is, "What is the message you want to convey to the people of the world through your *Star Wars* series films?"

LUCAS' G.S.

My main concept is, "What is the real power of God?" It's concentrated on the term, "Force." This is the pursuit of the concept of God's force, God's power, and in the end, what is God and what is anti-God, what is light and what is darkness.

Of course, it's reflected a lot of journalistic modern society, for example, you saw the *Episode IX*, the latest one, main figure is a young lady. It's just the reflection of the modern society, modern America, and the black person and the Asian lady, like that. But yeah, hmm, it'll be accepted by American Hollywood world, yeah, it's really, indeed, Hollywood-like world.

But at the beginning, it was quite different. I was not sure at that time, and no one could follow me. But in the end, it's made a great success, and I became very famous. So, this is another expression of what is God and what is devil. Yeah.

B
Thank you. As you just said about the real power of God, the real power from God, could you tell us more about the power of God, which is the Force in your *Star Wars* series?

LUCAS' G.S.
At the beginning, the Force, just the physical force I described, but now, *Episode IX*, the last one, it's included, for example, the healing power and the teleportation and the distance telepathy conversation. I added these additional powers. All are powers from God and it's told that the people who were sent by God and did great things in history have such kind of super powers.

So, in my meaning, I cannot imagine, for example, the Super Man-like, not-human power, but the hero should be a human but human with the power of divine within. That's the main point. So, "If you awaken to such kind of power, inner power," I presented to the people, especially for younger people or children that "you can be the next Jedi." It is my hope and the present to the next generation.

B
Thank you.

3

Star Wars Is the Reality of the Universe

SAYAKA OKAWA
Thank you for this precious opportunity. I have some questions. I heard that you were not the director of this *Episode IX*.

LUCAS' G.S.
Hmm... executive producer.[1]

SAYAKA OKAWA
And a different director made this movie. So, some of the fans said if you made *Episodes VII, VIII, IX*, your ending would have been different. What do you think about that?

LUCAS' G.S.
Hmm... Not so different, maybe. At first, it was a small movie and almost all of the story was written by me. But now, this *Star Wars* series has a very huge market, so there are gathering thousands of people. So, all the people gave

this piece a lot of talent of them. So, it's not the film of one person. People couldn't understand my word at first, but now there is the *Star Wars* world already in this universe and on this Earth. So, people are requiring about and imagining about such kind of *Star Wars* is essential or required or needed, like that.

So, quite different concepts are included. The heroes or heroines are quite different, so for example, ladies, black people, Asian people or some kind of space monsters, they are also the heroes and heroines.

They belong to Resistance, of course. But another side, the Empire is the famous Sith or Darth Vader, and now, Kylo Ren. These black-colored people and white clone-like armies just represent the China-like, how do you say, "the very huge, gigantic and totalitarian system and one dictatorship-like system" versus "Hong Kong-like resistance" struggling.

But it's very difficult for you. Is this the empire of China or empire of Iran? Yeah, they are also "men in black" and authoritarian country. So, the main point to distinguish between good and evil is in their mind, I mean, "How do they think about in their minds?" Is it successful or not, I don't know, I'm not sure, but people should feel about that.

C
Thank you for coming today. I would like to ask about your relationship with Stan Lee.

LUCAS' G.S.
Stan Lee? Oh.

C
Master mentioned that *Avengers* and *Star Wars* have similar themes. Do you know him in the Spirit World?

LUCAS' G.S.
Ah, Stan Lee. Hmm. Ah, yeah. Master Stan Lee. Yeah, I know. I know, I know, I know. Me, too. I'm another master, of course. Jedi Master, of course.

C
How did you come up with the idea of *Star Wars*? Where did the inspiration come from?

LUCAS' G.S.
Oh, this is just the real story, based on the real story. Reality of the universe. Yeah, in these billions of years. Yeah, it's true. It's a past and it's a future of you, and now.

Spiritual Interviews with the Guardian Spirit of George Lucas and the Spirit of Carrie Fisher

SAYAKA OKAWA

Some of the people said, "It would be the real story in the universe."

LUCAS' G.S.

Yeah. Yes.

SAYAKA OKAWA

Do you have any memories about *Star Wars*?

LUCAS' G.S.

Yeah, I'm just fighting like her... Rey? Princess, or no, Jedi to-be, Rey. Ah, you (Sayaka Okawa), almost you.

Yeah. And I saw Darth Vader-like person, Skywalker-like person, Leia-like person, the beginning of the evil, the First Order of the evil I experienced, I've heard about these stories, and still now, it's continuing in this universe. You, people who are living in bodies don't know about that, but spirits in the higher world were already informed about that reality.

B

You said that you experienced Star Wars of the universe, in reality.

LUCAS' G.S.
In reality, yeah.

B
Could you tell us more about the real Star Wars in this universe?

LUCAS' G.S.
Ah yeah. Star people have battleships like the Star Wars movie battleships and small ships which came from battleships and there are a lot of galaxies. And like a lot of countries on this Earth, they sometimes are battling. For example, the solar system people and another galaxy people sometimes made collision, and at that time there appeared a different messiah and he made what is the real direction of justice. It's like a Jedi Master.

There are a lot of Jedi Masters in this world and of course the master-like demons in this universe also, not only in this earthly world but another world, space world; evil spirits appear there sometimes. Sometimes, they came from another universe which we don't belong to. You sometimes say that it's a parallel world. In your earthly world, you live in the heavenly world and its dark side, hell world around the Earth, but when we look at the universe, there you can see a lot of galaxies and a lot of stars and we can see a lot of spaceships around this universe.

But there are some parts of the world which we cannot see. An invisible world, it might be the hidden part of the universe. It's a reverse-side of the universe. So, both are battling, I think so.

4
The Battle between the Light-Side and the Dark-Side

SAYAKA OKAWA
In our spiritual reading, we learned about the real darkside. There is a bad existence that's said to be Ahriman. I think it's similar to the Sith in *Star Wars*.

LUCAS' G.S.
Uh huh, yeah, yeah.

SAYAKA OKAWA
Do you know about the dark-side and the light-side well?

LUCAS' G.S.
It's a little difficult even for me. If I can tell the truth about that, I might be the Almighty God of the universe, so it's beyond my capacity. I know a little. Just the inspiration regarding movies to make films and had such kind of story. Yeah, there is a Sith-like Ahriman in this universe, but we cannot understand the whole figure or the system of the evil. It's very difficult. We need Jedi Master and

Planet Master and Galaxy Master, Messiah to know about that.

SAYAKA OKAWA
But in your movies, we can learn "How should we calm our mind," and for example, we can learn how the dark-side is from Anakin and Kylo Ren.

LUCAS' G.S.
Uh huh, yeah.

SAYAKA OKAWA
So, maybe you know how to control the mind and the difference between light spirit and dark-side. Could you tell us more deeply?

LUCAS' G.S.
Ah, it's regarding greed. People are apt to have greed and if that greed is concentrating on conquering other people or other country or planet, it sometimes becomes a gigantic evil, I think so. It's apt to do so.

But to protect yourself from this kind of greed, please know yourself, inner-self. Within you, there is harmony, I mean, this harmony comes from God. God's harmony can restore the balance of the universe. If evil-side, dark-side power becomes gigantic, you can make new balance to make yourself calm. You said *calm*. Yeah. And think good things only and get rid of the conquering desire for other people or other planets or other countries, and make harmony. Make the wavelength of your mind in tune with God's harmony. It's a harmony from pleasure, harmony from comfortableness, and harmony from happiness of the people.

So, the main concept of the war becomes "the gigantic empire's greed or endless desire" versus "conscience of the people," for example, Resistance people. God is a huge existence, but also, God is within each of you. So, if you can find the inner God within you, that God will reach other Gods of the other people, the web-like light circle will appear in the universe, and its light of web will wrap the dark power. So, this is the winning moment of God, I think so.

B
You said you are one of the Jedi Masters.

LUCAS' G.S.
[*Laughs.*] Small Jedi Master.

B
No, no, no. So, could you please teach us how to awaken to our spiritual power, I mean the power of the mind, and how to fight against evil existences in space?

LUCAS' G.S.
Hmm, ah, it's very difficult. Firstly, conquer your fear. It's the most terrible thing in the world and at the beginning of the lesson of life. When you grow up and want to have a good job or want to do a good job to help people or to add something good to this world, there will appear some kind of obstacles in front of you and you will hesitate and feel something dreadful and terrible thing. And you fear about that.

But your real success, your small success, one by one small success, will encourage you and will lead you to be a small master of your field. If you continue your job, you can be a great master. If you work harder and harder and 20 years or 30 years or 50 years have passed, after that, you'll be the Jedi Master-like person.

Jedi Masters use the lightsaber. The lightsaber is not real, but in another meaning, the lightsaber is a sword which divides your confusion and your indecisive attitude.

Spiritual Interview with the Guardian Spirit of George Lucas

You must make up your mind. You must see through what is right and what is evil. At that time, you need your lightsaber, and if you can use your lightsaber correctly, you can be one of the Jedi and the next Jedi Master. I think so. If you want to do a greater job, the obstacles also become greater and you need to be a professional master of the lightsaber. I think so.

B
Thank you.

*Spiritual Interviews with the Guardian Spirit of
George Lucas and the Spirit of Carrie Fisher*

5

Who Is Lucas' Spiritual Teacher?

C

I feel you have so much enlightenment about light and darkness. Whose teachings do you follow? Do you have a religion or a god or someone who teaches you about this?

LUCAS' G.S.

You ask me my teacher, spiritual teacher? My spiritual teacher, hmm. My spiritual teacher is known as Zarathustra in this earthly world. Yeah, it's a beginning of light and darkness. Yeah. It's very akin to me. I'm one part of Zarathustra, Zoroaster, I think so. I just feel a very serious relationship between that kind of Ahriman and Ahura Mazda-like struggling. Oh yeah, I was there at that time, indeed, and now I'm thinking about that.

The United States is also thinking about what is world justice, and so I described it in my movies. So, I have very keen attention to such kind of light sense and the sense of darkness, yeah. I'm one of the Jedi Masters of Zoroaster or Mani-like person. Not Jesus, but older than the age of Jesus Christ. I think so.

B
Now, we, Happy Science, are making the new animation film, *The Laws of the Universe*.

LUCAS' G.S.
Ah, yeah.

B
And it depicts the age of Elohim.

LUCAS' G.S.
Elohim. Hmm.

B
And, I suppose you have a relationship with God Elohim. Do you have any memories?

LUCAS' G.S.
I've heard about God Elohim, but He is the Supreme God, one of the Supreme Gods. It's beyond my powers, so I cannot recognize Him. I know His disciples.

B
Thank you.

*Spiritual Interviews with the Guardian Spirit of
George Lucas and the Spirit of Carrie Fisher*

SAYAKA OKAWA
So, you have a deep connection with Zoroaster?

LUCAS' G.S.
Yeah.

SAYAKA OKAWA
What kind of connection do you have?

LUCAS' G.S.
I'm one of the aides of Zoroaster. For example, in this world, you have a lot of judges and prosecutors-like people. We also have such kind of people in the heavenly world, and they are searching for the good or bad of every person, especially the people with leadership.

For example, if I were in charge of legal matters, like Carlos Ghosn's escape from Japan[2] is evil or not, good or not. Japanese people think, "That's a bad thing." Lebanon people think, "It's good." And, French people think, "80 percent is good. Carlos Ghosn should escape from Japan. Japan is a very black legal society, so as soon as possible, he will escape from Japan. Japan is underdeveloped and takes a very special attitude toward the people who made great success. It's another case of envy about the successful people, so it's not neutral." They think so. So now, today, Lebanon Jedi Master, French Jedi Master, American Jedi Master, and Japanese Jedi Master are *chanbara*-ing[3] now, yeah. [*Laughs.*]

6

Influence from Kurosawa and Lucas' Past Lives

B

You were just talking about the *chanbara* among the Jedi Masters' countries. I suppose you have some relation with Japan since you respect Mr. Kurosawa.

LUCAS' G.S.

Ah, yes.

B

Akira Kurosawa, you respect him very much. Do you have any memory about the reincarnation in Japan?

LUCAS' G.S.

Yeah, I received a lot of influence from Mr. Akira Kurosawa. I like the samurai sword, and Darth Vader wearing the *kabuto* (warrior helmet) of Japan. Oriental mystery, yeah, indeed.

But in the ancient age, maybe I was born in some place of Asia, and was a soldier and played sword. I worked very hard, studied very hard, and practiced very hard to be a master of sword. I'm not correct in my memory, but it's Japan or Korea or China. It's confusing, but I did some kind of sword player in the Asian area. When we live in the Christian society, we don't think about too much regarding past lives, so I'm not sure about that. Maybe in Far East Asia I was born, and before that I was born in Iran or Iraq area, and at that time, I was a disciple of Zoroaster, maybe. Maybe one of the prosecutors of him, but it's not so sure.

SAYAKA OKAWA
Then, your movies have been influenced by Japanese bushido and maybe Zen. You are also interested in Buddhism and Japanese bushido. For example, *Jedi* comes from the Japanese word *jidai* (time) and Padme Amidala's name comes from *Amidabutsu* (Amitabha Buddha), so you love the oriental world, I think.

LUCAS' G.S.
Yeah.

Spiritual Interviews with the Guardian Spirit of
George Lucas and the Spirit of Carrie Fisher

SAYAKA OKAWA
Do you know about Buddhism and Japanese bushido?

LUCAS' G.S.
Oh, it's just *Shaka-ni-seppo* (lit. "Preaching to the Buddha," a Japanese proverb that means "to teach someone something that they already know well."). So, I cannot tell correctly about Buddhism or *satori*, enlightenment of the Japanese. So, hmm... but I can feel, I can feel, I can feel, yeah. I can feel bushido and I can feel Zen Buddhism, Zen spirit, but if I try to express it correctly in words, it's very difficult and in vain, I think.

It's... just emptiness, yeah, emptiness. Seek for emptiness, and you can reach the reality. If you seek for reality, you can just see emptiness. Emptiness is the reality and reality is emptiness. People just can see only the colors and the bodies and the materials, but these are in vain, these are vanity. Please look through this vanity, perish your illusion, and just seek for emptiness, and you can reach your reality.

Your reality is some kind of light, but to tell the truth, light is not the reality. Go beyond the light, there is nothing. Nothing is the beginning. Beginning is just inside the great Buddha's belly. That's the beginning. It's dark, but it's dark, but it's bright. Bright, but it's dark. Oh, it's the beginning and to join in the beginning of the Buddha's belly is the enlightenment, I think so.

SAYAKA OKAWA
Thank you very much.

Spiritual Interviews with the Guardian Spirit of George Lucas and the Spirit of Carrie Fisher

7

Promoting People's Awakening to the Space Age

C

What is the mission of George Lucas in this lifetime? Do you have a quick message to him as his guardian spirit?

LUCAS' G.S.

His mission is, one is to promote the awakening of the people. There will come the space age and it just started. Me, and of course, Spielberg also are warning people. "We are entering the space age, so please prepare for this space age." These are the meaning of our movies. One is this point.

Another one is, when you watch my movies, you will see the future society-like people and machine and war, and in another part, you'll see the olden-age warriors or creatures, monsters. So, in my movies, the future style and the ancient style are mixed, but it's a reality of the universe.

In this universe, you just think about [*pointing to his watch*] this kind of watch-like time; "time flies like an arrow, straightly," you want to think like that, but in reality, the time of this universe is spiraling, and in some meaning, it's the ancient age and in some meaning, it's the future. So, sometimes we are confused, "Is this the ancient age or the future age, or are we just in the air of the wheels of time and space?" It's very difficult. We have different times in this universe, I think so.

So, as you already received some kind of space people's messages, they lived for example, 100 million years ago, but the people who lived 100 million years ago can teach us. Oh, it's incredible. And, you can send your message to the people who will live 100 million years in the future. So, the real Force of God, I mean telepathy and beyond telepathy, super telepathy, God's telepathy can reach beyond hundreds of millions of years ago and ahead, both.

So, "real God or real Buddha is living in what age," we cannot acknowledge about that. But our space and our time are in the great wheel of the universe. So, we, human beings or human being spirits cannot understand the whole image of the world.

You have some question about that? Yeah, you can just go send your voice to the people in the olden-age. Ah, yeah.

Spiritual Interviews with the Guardian Spirit of
George Lucas and the Spirit of Carrie Fisher

SAYAKA OKAWA

Thank you. I have one more question. Maybe you have a lot of inspiration from the universe. In your movies, there are a lot of aliens. So, how should we get great inspiration like you? Could you please teach us?

LUCAS' G.S.

Hmm, yeah. Think and think and think and think and thinking.

SAYAKA OKAWA

But our alien reading has revealed the existence of an alien similar to Chewbacca. There really exists, so maybe you...

LUCAS' G.S.

Oh, yeah. Bigfoot. He is Bigfoot. Yeah, inspiration.

SAYAKA OKAWA

Your inspirations come from the real universe.

LUCAS' G.S.

In some meaning, yes. In another meaning, it's imagination. For example, [*pointing to B*] look at him.

Hmm... some kind of elephant-like space people can be seen through him, yeah. White, long-nosed, very fat, great ears, and *noshi-noshi* (slow and heavy) walking. Yeah, you can imagine and write or describe that picture, and there will appear a space alien. And, when I look at you (Sayaka Okawa), I can see Jedi Rey. But sometimes, you think like, umm... it's a taboo, so umm...

SAYAKA OKAWA
Pig?

LUCAS' G.S.
Pig [*laughs*] [*audience laughs*]. Yeah, pig-like, but it's not so good idea, so yeah, another one. Yeah. Some kind of pet I imagine, but you can be a Rey-like woman warrior.

Yeah, it's an imagination, but what I can imagine means God also imagined, long long ago. If people or people's spirits can imagine, God already imagined that kind of creatures. God made creatures of the universe by imagination, so if I can imagine, God can imagine and God can create such kind of creatures.

I made a lot of creatures. Some of them are reality, other ones are just imagination, but in this universe, there

Spiritual Interviews with the Guardian Spirit of
George Lucas and the Spirit of Carrie Fisher

will be alive such kind of creatures, I think. I don't want to say about you. I imagine some kind of animal, but I can't say about that, sorry.

8

I Might Be the "Pre-advice" of the Great Savior

B

The time is almost up. I have two more questions, so could you please answer them?

LUCAS' G.S.
OK.

B

Last night, the spirit of Ms. Carrie Fisher said, "George Lucas is quite impressive, a disguised God." I suppose you are a part of savior because Stan Lee, your friend, is a part of Zeus according to Happy Science readings.

LUCAS' G.S.
Ah, really.

B

And I suppose you also are a part of savior. Could you...

Spiritual Interviews with the Guardian Spirit of George Lucas and the Spirit of Carrie Fisher

LUCAS' G.S.
Ah, no, no, no.

B
If possible, could you please...

LUCAS' G.S.
Savior means "saving money"?

B
[*Laughs.*] No, not saving.

LUCAS' G.S.
Yeah, yeah, in some meaning, it's true. I experienced a lot of difficulties in saving money. To be a savior is good, yeah, indeed.

B
In other words, I suppose you are a great angel or a great Jedi Master.

Spiritual Interview with the Guardian Spirit of George Lucas

LUCAS' G.S.

It's an imagination. It's just my imagination. I'm old enough, 75 years old, so my passion and my strength have been weakened. This is… yeah, oh, I'm making another movie, *Indiana Jones 5*, so my last day will be coming.

Stan Lee is a god because he can live to 95 years old. Oh, he's a monster. I cannot imagine. I cannot live such a long-time. In my younger days, I made great efforts to succeed in my mission of making films, but I'm not so strong in my mind. So, the strong warriors are my desire or the shadows of my desire. In reality, I'm not so strong a person like the Jedi. But the people of the world helped me a lot, so I was known by them. I might be just the "pre-advice" of the coming of the Great Savior of the next age. Yeah, I think so.

Spiritual Interviews with the Guardian Spirit of
George Lucas and the Spirit of Carrie Fisher

9

What He Hopes for Future Space Movies

B

OK, thank you. This is my last question. Could you give a message to all the fans of the world?

LUCAS' G.S.

All the fans of the world? It's difficult. All the fans of the... My series will end, but time flies like an arrow, and if 50 years pass, within 50 years, the mechanical system and the making system of creating movies will be quite different, and my movies, also, will be outdated at that time, so please follow the "new George Lucas" and make the next space movie. I hope so.

At that day, at that age, you will receive a lot of information from space people. It's a space age. You can get different information from space people. And, please add that element and make great Jedi or Jedi Masters.

If I make in the near future—it's just my imagination— the next Jedi should make teleportation to another galaxy and *chanbara* at that star. My movies need a lot money and almost 90 percent of the movies are on the set, so please make more spiritual pictures like *The Laws of the Universe*. I want to watch your next animation movie, yeah.

SAYAKA OKAWA
We are making the new universal movie.

LUCAS' G.S.
Ah, you are writing a synopsis.

SAYAKA OKAWA
Yes. We are making *The Laws of the Universe II* (aforementioned), and we are now planning to make *III*. So, could you give us some advice to make good movies?

LUCAS' G.S.
Ah, you have the tendency of not wanting to kill people or battle scenes. In the United States, especially Hollywood, people want to watch scenes of mass murder, so the direction or the appreciation points are quite different. If you don't like killing millions of people, you can just describe the mentality of the inner soul.

But we, American people, easily want to make a war and kill tens of thousands of people easily, but in reality, it's not suitable for modern Japanese people. So, if you want to get an American welcome, you must kill a lot of people. But if you don't like such kind of taste, please disregard them, and you should go your own way.

SAYAKA OKAWA
OK, thank you so much.

B
Thank you very much, the guardian spirit of George Lucas.

LUCAS' G.S.
It's OK? Thank you very much. Have a good job. Bye-bye.

B
Thank you very much, Master Okawa.

ENDNOTES

1 Lucas is not officially so, but is credited for the characters he created. Also, the director met and discussed with him before writing the screenplay.

2 Carlos Ghosn was the chairman and CEO of the Renault-Nissan-Mitsubishi Alliance, a strategic partnership among those automotive manufacturers. He was arrested in Japan in November 2018, on allegations of under-reporting his salary and gross misuse of company assets. Ghosn fled from Japan to Lebanon in December 2019, breaking his bail conditions.

3 chanbara means "sword fight"

EXTRA CHAPTER

Spiritual Interview with the Guardian Spirit of Leonardo DiCaprio

*Recorded in Japanese on December 26, 2019
in the Special Lecture Hall of Happy Science in Japan.*

Leonardo DiCaprio (1974 - Present)

An American actor. He appeared in many TV commercials since his early teens and made his first movie appearance in the 1991 movie, *Critters 3*. He made a breakthrough in 1993 after co-starring with Robert De Niro in *This Boy's Life*. DiCaprio established himself as a star after playing the lead role in the 1997 megahit movie, *Titanic*, which was a record box office at the time. He went on to play many other roles and eventually won his first Academy Award for Best Actor in the 2015 movie, *The Revenant*, after being nominated for the fourth time.

Interviewers from Happy Science*

Shio Okawa
　Aide to Master & CEO

Sayaka Okawa
　Vice Chairperson,
　Chief of CEO's Office,
　Religious Affairs Headquarters

---

* The professional titles represent their position at the time of the interview.

*Spiritual Interviews with the Guardian Spirit of
George Lucas and the Spirit of Carrie Fisher*

1

Spiritual Secrets of Leonardo DiCaprio

DiCaprio's guardian spirit
frowns to a particular phrase

[Editor's Note: The original song by Master Ryuho Okawa, "Wanderer" is playing in the background.]

LEONARDO DICAPRIO'S GUARDIAN SPIRIT
Hah, huff. Ah, ah, ah...

SHIO OKAWA
Who is it?

DICAPRIO'S G.S.
DiCaprio.

SHIO OKAWA
Mr. DiCaprio!?

Spiritual Interview with the Guardian Spirit of Leonardo DiCaprio

DICAPRIO'S G.S.
Hmm?

SHIO OKAWA
Because we watched it [The movie, *Titanic* starring DiCaprio]?

DICAPRIO'S G.S.
Hmm. You don't like me coming?

SHIO OKAWA
"Don't like me coming"?

DICAPRIO'S G.S.
No?

SHIO OKAWA
Oh, you mean, for a spiritual message?

SAYAKA OKAWA
Because we rejected him once.

*Spiritual Interviews with the Guardian Spirit of
George Lucas and the Spirit of Carrie Fisher*

SHIO OKAWA
Really?

SAYAKA OKAWA
Ms. X rejected him, saying, "We don't need him. He's over the hill."

DICAPRIO'S G.S.
Hmm!

SHIO OKAWA
That's not true.

DICAPRIO'S G.S.
I'll frown, of course.

SHIO OKAWA
Anyway, you can speak Japanese?

DICAPRIO'S G.S.
I grew popular when she was born, so it's her who came late.

SHIO OKAWA
You're right.

Spiritual Interview with the Guardian Spirit of Leonardo DiCaprio

Have the victims of Titanic gone up to heaven?

SHIO OKAWA
I'm getting a very heavy vibe. Is there anybody else there?

DICAPRIO'S G.S.
Hmm, over a thousand victims of Titanic.

SHIO OKAWA
Oh, is that why it's heavy?

DICAPRIO'S G.S.
Yes. They all want you to lead them to heaven.

SHIO OKAWA
I see. You mean, they haven't gone up to heaven yet.

DICAPRIO'S G.S.
Of course not. It was terrifying, you know? It was a hell of terror because less than half could survive.

SHIO OKAWA
You can speak Japanese?

*Spiritual Interviews with the Guardian Spirit of
George Lucas and the Spirit of Carrie Fisher*

DICAPRIO'S G.S.
I wonder why I can. It's odd.

SHIO OKAWA
It really is.

DICAPRIO'S G.S.
Do I need to speak in English? But I'd feel sorry for you, so I'm speaking in Japanese.

SHIO OKAWA
Ah, you are kind. Thank you very much.

DICAPRIO'S G.S.
Hmm. You don't want to talk in English, do you?

SHIO OKAWA
Well, Japanese would be better.

DICAPRIO'S G.S.
Yes, yes. I thought so. Because, you know, Japanese is now an international language. Japan is the center of the world.

Spiritual Interview with the Guardian Spirit of Leonardo DiCaprio

SHIO OKAWA
Really?

DICAPRIO'S G.S.
Yes.

SHIO OKAWA
Why?

DICAPRIO'S G.S.
Because there is Happy Science.

SHIO OKAWA
You, Mr. DiCaprio know El Cantare?

DICAPRIO'S G.S.
I know Him. Of course, I know Him.

SHIO OKAWA
You know...

DICAPRIO'S G.S.
I know.

Spiritual Interviews with the Guardian Spirit of
George Lucas and the Spirit of Carrie Fisher

SHIO OKAWA
That is amazing.

Connection between DiCaprio's guardian spirit and God Odin

SHIO OKAWA
So, we feel like we are losing our energy because we watched *Titanic*?

DICAPRIO'S G.S.
Yes, that's one reason. Also, it crashed into the iceberg and sank, and I have a memory of icebergs. You know, the savior in the north you talk about…

SHIO OKAWA
Odin (the chief god of Scandinavia).

DICAPRIO'S G.S.
Odin?

Spiritual Interview with the Guardian Spirit of Leonardo DiCaprio

SHIO OKAWA
Yes.

DICAPRIO'S G.S.
I was there at the time of God Odin (about 8,000 to 9,000 years ago), so I know....

SHIO OKAWA
He says he was there at the time of God Odin.

SAYAKA OKAWA
Yes.

DICAPRIO'S G.S.
That's why I have a memory. An iceberg appeared in that movie, and I feel something from it.

SHIO OKAWA
I see.

DICAPRIO'S G.S.
Because I served God Odin.

Spiritual Interviews with the Guardian Spirit of
George Lucas and the Spirit of Carrie Fisher

SHIO OKAWA

Oh, my! He says he served God Odin.

DICAPRIO'S G.S.

That's why I know Him.

SHIO OKAWA

He says that's why he knows El Cantare.

DICAPRIO'S G.S.

That's right. I worked a lot. I hunted polar bears, reindeer or deer, and captured beavers. I worked very hard.

SAYAKA OKAWA

That's why you often act in movies about hunters…

DICAPRIO'S G.S.

That's right.

SHIO OKAWA

And then you acted in *The Revenant* (Twentieth Century Fox, 2015).

Spiritual Interview with the Guardian Spirit of Leonardo DiCaprio

DICAPRIO'S G.S.
Because I experienced it. So, I know well about cold places.

SHIO OKAWA
You like cold places.

DICAPRIO'S G.S.
Well, I know warm places also, but I remember experiencing a cold place in my past life.

SHIO OKAWA
Then, your deepest connection is with God Odin?

DICAPRIO'S G.S.
And, he's been popular recently, you know, "God Moomin."

SHIO OKAWA
Moomin.

DICAPRIO'S G.S.
Yes. That is God Odin in disguise.

Spiritual Interviews with the Guardian Spirit of
George Lucas and the Spirit of Carrie Fisher

SHIO OKAWA
It is?

DICAPRIO'S G.S.
Yes. God Odin takes such form to appear in the modern world. Just like how you change into a panda.

SHIO OKAWA
I see. You know that I am a "panda"?

DICAPRIO'S G.S.
Yeah. You are famous.

SHIO OKAWA
[*Laughs.*] In the Spirit World?

DICAPRIO'S G.S.
Famous. The panda is a famous character in the Spirit World.

SHIO OKAWA
I see.

Spiritual Interview with the Guardian Spirit of Leonardo DiCaprio

If DiCaprio were to appear in a Happy Science movie

DICAPRIO'S G.S.
I wish you will make a movie for me to act in.

SHIO OKAWA
Just your casting fee would cost millions of dollars.

DICAPRIO'S G.S.
But it wouldn't happen if I'm over the hill, I guess.

SHIO OKAWA
You are not. You are still cool.

DICAPRIO'S G.S.
If you would cast me as Odin, I can act.

SHIO OKAWA
I see. OK.

DICAPRIO'S G.S.
I can act a role like that.

SHIO OKAWA

OK, I will keep that in mind.

DICAPRIO'S G.S.

OK? I want to act as Odin. But I wasn't born in cold places only. I was born in the south, also.

SHIO OKAWA

I can understand that, since your Japanese is excellent.

DICAPRIO'S G.S.

Yes. I was actually there at the time of King Ra Mu, too (see *Kokai Reigen Cho Kodai Bunmei Mu no Daio Ra Mu no Honshin* [lit. "Publicly Recorded Spiritual Messages from Ra Mu, the Great King of Super Ancient Civilization of Mu"]).

SHIO OKAWA

Then, do you know Ms. Sayaka?

DICAPRIO'S G.S.

I know her. She was a princess.

Spiritual Interview with the Guardian Spirit of Leonardo DiCaprio

SAYAKA OKAWA
Hmm. What were you doing at the time?

SHIO OKAWA
Where were you at that time?

DICAPRIO'S G.S.
I was a knight, of course.

SHIO OKAWA
A knight?

DICAPRIO'S G.S.
A knight.

SHIO OKAWA
That is amazing, Mr. DiCaprio.

DICAPRIO'S G.S.
I was, certainly. You shouldn't think that knights are in your group only.

SHIO OKAWA
I agree. That makes sense.

*Spiritual Interviews with the Guardian Spirit of
George Lucas and the Spirit of Carrie Fisher*

DICAPRIO'S G.S.

Now, you are putting effort in entertainment. DiCaprio himself is still not aware of it, but I already recognize your activities, so I hope we will cross paths someday.

SHIO OKAWA

Thank you very much.

DICAPRIO'S G.S.

But since you are growing rapidly, his life will cross paths with yours in the near future. John Lennon is already dead, so even though he... but I'm still alive.

If we can become friends somewhere, you know, if I can become friends with Happy Science's moviemaking people, good things can happen.

Spiritual Interview with the Guardian Spirit of Leonardo DiCaprio

How DiCaprio was able to win an Academy Award with the movie, *The Revenant*

SHIO OKAWA
This time, we are aiming to win the Academy Award... with the movie, *Immortal Hero* (executive producer Ryuho Okawa, released in 2019), so please support us.

DICAPRIO'S G.S.
I hope we can meet. I really hope to meet you.

SHIO OKAWA
We would be glad if you could watch the movie somewhere.

DICAPRIO'S G.S.
You can make connections easily if you are like an acquaintance, a relative, or a friend of DiCaprio.

SHIO OKAWA
Well, that's true.

DICAPRIO'S G.S.
Right? So...

Spiritual Interviews with the Guardian Spirit of
George Lucas and the Spirit of Carrie Fisher

SHIO OKAWA

If you would please give that inspiration to the living Mr. DiCaprio...

DICAPRIO'S G.S.

You've got friends (in the Spirit World) like Keira Knightley, Natalie Portman, and Cate Blanchett, right? So, you can say you are friends with DiCaprio as well.

SHIO OKAWA

I see. Great! [*Applauds.*]

DICAPRIO'S G.S.

Japanese actors won't get you to the Academy Award. They rarely will.

SHIO OKAWA

It's quite difficult.

DICAPRIO'S G.S.

Will I be able to appear in your movie someday as a blue-eyed samurai or king [*laughs*]? Maybe someday, I can appear if you spend about 300 million dollars on a movie.

Spiritual Interview with the Guardian Spirit of Leonardo DiCaprio

SHIO OKAWA

[*Laughs.*] Please give that inspiration to the living Mr. DiCaprio...

DICAPRIO'S G.S.

Hmm, the living DiCaprio would be nothing if he is labeled "an old guy over the hill" as Ms. X said.

SHIO OKAWA

That is not true.

DICAPRIO'S G.S.

I've already grown past the age for romance. Anyway, yes.

SHIO OKAWA

But recently, you received an Academy Award with *The Revenant* (at the time of this recording).

DICAPRIO'S G.S.

I did, in the role of an outcast. But that was true because I really experienced it.

Spiritual Interviews with the Guardian Spirit of
George Lucas and the Spirit of Carrie Fisher

DiCaprio's G.S. and
the Spirit World he belongs to

SHIO OKAWA
Do you have a name?

DICAPRIO'S G.S.
Guardian...

SHIO OKAWA
Can we spiritually connect to you if we call for "Mr. Leo"?

DICAPRIO'S G.S.
Hmm. I have many different kinds of names, so it's... Anyway, it is not true that only female actors are great. It's impossible.

SHIO OKAWA
You mean, there are great male actors, also.

DICAPRIO'S G.S.
There must be, also. As your friends. I have a stronger connection with the spirit world of creative people, the world of creativity and beauty. I am one of your friendly

angels. So, as long as you are making movies and growing worldwide, we will definitely cross paths somewhere.

It would be great if we could be friends. Since Stan Lee has already returned to heaven, I hope I could be of some help. I don't think I'm inferior to Natalie Portman in spiritual level.

SHIO OKAWA
That is incredible!

DICAPRIO'S G.S.
Yes. She is in the spiritual world of Israel, which is small. But I am worldwide, since I have been born in various countries. I had spiritual connections with Odin, Ra Mu, and Hermes. So, we have often crossed paths. That's why I get excited when you are doing remarkable work. It makes me a bit excited. I want to help you in some way.

SHIO OKAWA
I'm happy to hear that.

DICAPRIO'S G.S.
I hope I can help you with something to introduce you to the world. I wish we could make some connection.

People in Japanese entertainment wouldn't make any connections with you, and they only run away, right? They think a bad rumor about them will spread if they make connections with religions. But I don't think it is right. There must be a deep connection between religion and entertainment.

So, if you become famous as artists, we might cross paths somewhere. At the earliest, we might meet next February (at the Academy Awards ceremony).

SHIO OKAWA
[*Laughs.*]

DICAPRIO'S G.S.
That might be a long shot. I don't know. I'm sorry to say that I still don't have enough power to support you.

SHIO OKAWA
But we are very glad.

Spiritual Interview with the Guardian Spirit of Leonardo DiCaprio

DICAPRIO'S G.S.
DiCaprio knows that you are active in the entertainment industry. So, I'm saying, "Quick! Come on and join us!" "Come to America!"

*Spiritual Interviews with the Guardian Spirit of
George Lucas and the Spirit of Carrie Fisher*

2

Becoming Famous Worldwide

Movies and entertainment have the power to make you famous worldwide

DICAPRIO'S G.S.
To have the people in the world watch your movies, you need to use leverage, otherwise it's impossible. Making your movies worldwide would be a great power to make you a world religion, in this modern world.

Titanic was not such a big deal, just a love story on a sinking ship. But Happy Science, Master Ryuho Okawa, and El Cantare definitely need to become famous worldwide, so in order to make them known in the world, many people are...

SHIO OKAWA
Thinking hard?

DICAPRIO'S G.S.
Thinking hard. So, they will surely connect with you at some point. When your activities expand into many

areas, you will meet people in various fields that have connections with you.

Nowadays, entertainers can be famous worldwide, unlike in the older days. A branch spirit of Jesus was born as John Lennon, you know, so I don't know how great DiCaprio would be then, but it wouldn't be surprising if he was an angel, right?

SHIO OKAWA
Right.

DICAPRIO'S G.S.
If you become famous in the Japanese movie industry only, you will just be one of the Japanese ethnic gods, so you should work to be known more widely.

So, I want to start something that will create a chance for you because I am a follower of Odin, Hermes, and Ra Mu.

SHIO OKAWA
I see. Thank you very much.

DICAPRIO'S G.S.
Thanks for buying Moomin goods.

SHIO OKAWA

Moomin [*laughs*]. We also connected through Moomin.

DICAPRIO'S G.S.

Yes, yes. I was in Moominvalley as well.

SHIO OKAWA

I see.

DICAPRIO'S G.S.

Yes.

Through art and music, convey to people that the Great One was born

SHIO OKAWA

Then, we would appreciate it if you and Mr. DiCaprio would give us advice when we make movies.

DICAPRIO'S G.S.

Sure. You can have him meet you at some point. And, I can do something for you as a spiritual adviser in making movies, though you need to be able to get in and out of Hollywood if you hope to meet DiCaprio himself. But if you keep hoping for it, it will come nearer to you, so please keep it in mind.

There are people far and near, and I'm not far. I'm near. Now, I'm not with you, but I have the desire to help you at some point even though I may be "an old man over the hill."

SHIO OKAWA
I don't think so.

SAYAKA OKAWA
[*Laughs.*] We are sorry.

DICAPRIO'S G.S.
It hurt me. She shouldn't say such words to a star.

SAYAKA OKAWA
I agree.

SHIO OKAWA
We were watching *Titanic* just now, and you were splendid, Mr. Leo.

Spiritual Interviews with the Guardian Spirit of
George Lucas and the Spirit of Carrie Fisher

DICAPRIO'S G.S.
Really? Thank you.

SAYAKA OKAWA
You took the world by storm with that act.

SHIO OKAWA
It was the No. 1 all-time box-office record in the world for a long time.

DICAPRIO'S G.S.
Hmm, awards were mainly for the movie itself, though. My acting was not much different from *Romeo+Juliet*.

SHIO OKAWA
But it should have been quite difficult to be world-famous for such beauty as a male actor, not a female actor.

DICAPRIO'S G.S.
It's tough to make influence on the world, certainly. But you, also, have to do it now. You've got to make influence on the world. You need to be more famous. Not for bad things.

Spiritual Interview with the Guardian Spirit of Leonardo DiCaprio

SHIO OKAWA
For good things.

DICAPRIO'S G.S.
I think you need to be famous through being praised. You know, it's like... you must hit a home run. You seem to stick to hitting singles, but you should hit a home run. You've got to hit a homer. (Otherwise) you won't be famous. You must become world-famous.

Japan seems to be trying hard to hide you, despite the fact that the Great One was born. That's a pity. It is a pity.

SHIO OKAWA
It really is sinful.

DICAPRIO'S G.S.
I believe it's a pity.

Well, although Mr. Trump had been known as a real estate tycoon, he became world-famous as the American president. But I believe he (Master Ryuho Okawa) is more than that, so you need to have more people know that the Lord has been born while He is alive. And that's why art and music are necessary.

Spiritual Interviews with the Guardian Spirit of
George Lucas and the Spirit of Carrie Fisher

I have many friends in the Spirit World, so I will try to get them, angels of beauty and angels of art, together and support you.

SHIO OKAWA
Thank you very much.

DICAPRIO'S G.S.
It's sad to see Japanese no-name actors avoid appearing in your movies because you are a religion, and the mass media ignoring you. So, I am hoping to help you in the near future.

SHIO OKAWA
Thank you very much in advance. We will also do our best.

"I want to give advice to your entertainment sections"

DICAPRIO'S G.S.
I have so many things I'm thinking about, but this situation is not so good. We cannot talk for long...

Spiritual Interview with the Guardian Spirit of Leonardo DiCaprio

SHIO OKAWA
Should we have had an official spiritual interview?

DICAPRIO'S G.S.
Yes, it needs to be an official one. Maybe this situation is not good.

I hope I can give some advice to your entertainment sections next time.

SHIO OKAWA
OK.

DICAPRIO'S G.S.
It might be better for me to give spiritual messages in English.

Anyway, I hope you will become bigger. You know, I would become a Happy Science believer in America. That might make you famous.

SHIO OKAWA
That's true.

Spiritual Interviews with the Guardian Spirit of
George Lucas and the Spirit of Carrie Fisher

DICAPRIO'S G.S.
I'm an old man over the hill, though.

SHIO OKAWA
No, you are not.

DICAPRIO'S G.S.
Ha, that makes my blood boil. I cannot forgive her.

SAYAKA OKAWA
[*Laughs.*] True.

SHIO OKAWA
[*Laughs.*]

DICAPRIO'S G.S.
It's against the teachings of Truth, I guess?

SHIO OKAWA
You came here because Master once said, "We can record spiritual messages from DiCaprio's guardian spirit," right?

Spiritual Interview with the Guardian Spirit of Leonardo DiCaprio

SAYAKA OKAWA
He (DiCaprio's G.S.) came here before.

SHIO OKAWA
Ah, did he?

SAYAKA OKAWA
I think it was after Master watched *The Revenant*.

SHIO OKAWA
Ah, yes, yes, yes. You are right. But we said no.

SAYAKA OKAWA
That's right.

SHIO OKAWA
We are sorry.

DICAPRIO'S G.S.
I suddenly feel old because I was called "an old man over the hill."

*Spiritual Interviews with the Guardian Spirit of
George Lucas and the Spirit of Carrie Fisher*

SHIO OKAWA
You are not. Please keep shining.

Messages from DiCaprio's G.S.

DICAPRIO'S G.S.
Natalie Portman, Keira Knightley, and Japan's Shio Okawa are the three great beauties of the world.

SHIO OKAWA
No, no, no [*laughs*]. No, no. You are too kind.

DICAPRIO'S G.S.
Three great beauties.

SHIO OKAWA
That is not true.

DICAPRIO'S G.S.
So, that's why you must give it your best shot.
　Anyway, I just wanted to say that I have a connection to Moominvalley.

Spiritual Interview with the Guardian Spirit of Leonardo DiCaprio

SHIO OKAWA

All right, then, maybe we can have another spiritual interview with you.

DICAPRIO'S G.S.

Odin. Odin was the key in the movie, *Thor*. So, we can make, not another Thor movie, but a movie about Odin's myth.

SHIO OKAWA

That is true. You mean, we can ask you about God Odin, right?

DICAPRIO'S G.S.

Yes. You might need to film in Hokkaido for that. Hahaha [*laughs*].

SHIO OKAWA & SAYAKA OKAWA

[*Laugh.*]

DICAPRIO'S G.S.

Haha [*laughs*].

SHIO OKAWA
We can do an animation.

DICAPRIO'S G.S.
I don't think we can do it at the North Pole.

SHIO OKAWA
How about animation?

DICAPRIO'S G.S.
Ah, that's good. It's too old to find any historical records on it, but there are ones who can tell you about it, of course.

SHIO OKAWA
I see. We would appreciate it.

DICAPRIO'S G.S.
I remember fighting at that time. I hunted animals, also.

Anyway, you have many, many other friends here and there, so you must uncover them. Hollywood is still very far, high, and unreachable, but it's not such a big deal. Compared to the great civilizations created by Odin,

Hermes, or Ra Mu, it's much, much lower. So, I hope you have a stronger mind, a grander perspective, and a bigger hope.

SHIO OKAWA
Yes. Thank you very much.

DICAPRIO'S G.S.
If you want some advice in entertainment, please ask me again.

SHIO OKAWA
Yes! Absolutely. We appreciate it. Thank you very much.

RYUHO OKAWA
He came here in a proper way after we watched the movie.

Afterword

These are spiritual messages spoken by me in English, so the content is easy to understand. If the English is too difficult for you, you can just read the Japanese translation.

We are trying to release the Japanese version of Star Wars as The Laws of the Universe. I hope it reaches the people all over the world. I heard there are Happy Science members in 164 countries now, so I would be happy if each country can screen The Laws of the Universe (this time, Part 2).

A famous producer and actors of Hollywood are supporting us spiritually. It is an honor, so firstly, I want to create a large boom in Japan, then spread it to America and Europe and all over the world. As the Master of the masters (the Most Enlightened One), I want to include the truth of the universe in my enlightenment this time.

Ryuho Okawa
Master & CEO of Happy Science Group
Aug. 14, 2021

ABOUT THE AUTHOR

RYUHO OKAWA was born on July 7th 1956, in Tokushima, Japan. After graduating from the University of Tokyo with a law degree, he joined a Tokyo-based trading house. While working at its New York headquarters, he studied international finance at the Graduate Center of the City University of New York. In 1981, he attained Great Enlightenment and became aware that he is El Cantare with a mission to bring salvation to all humankind. In 1986, he established Happy Science. It now has members in over 160 countries across the world, with more than 700 local branches and temples as well as 10,000 missionary houses around the world. The total number of lectures has exceeded 3,300 (of which more than 150 are in English) and over 2,850 books (of which more than 600 are Spiritual Interview Series) have been published, many of which are translated into 37 languages. Many of the books, including *The Laws of the Sun* have become best sellers or million sellers. To date, Happy Science has produced 23 movies. The original story and original concept were given by the Executive Producer Ryuho Okawa. Recent movie titles are *Beautiful Lure–A Modern Tale of "Painted Skin"* (live-action, May 2021), *Into the Dreams... and Horror Experiences* (live-action, August 2021), and *The Laws of the Universe–The Age of Elohim* (animation movie scheduled to be released in October of 2021). He has also composed the lyrics and music of over 450 songs, such as theme songs and featured songs of movies. Moreover, he is the Founder of Happy Science University and Happy Science Academy (Junior and Senior High School), Founder and President of the Happiness Realization Party, Founder and Honorary Headmaster of Happy Science Institute of Government and Management, Founder of IRH Press Co., Ltd., and the Chairperson of NEW STAR PRODUCTION Co., Ltd. and ARI Production Co., Ltd.

WHAT IS EL CANTARE?

El Cantare means "the Light of the Earth," and is the Supreme God of the Earth who has been guiding humankind since the beginning of Genesis. He is whom Jesus called Father and Muhammad called Allah, and is the Creator in Shintoism, *Ame-no-Mioya-Gami*. Different parts of El Cantare's core consciousness have descended to Earth in the past, once as Alpha and another as Elohim. His branch spirits, such as Shakyamuni Buddha and Hermes, have descended to Earth many times and helped to flourish many civilizations. To unite various religions and to integrate various fields of study in order to build a new civilization on Earth, a part of the core consciousness has descended to Earth as Master Ryuho Okawa.

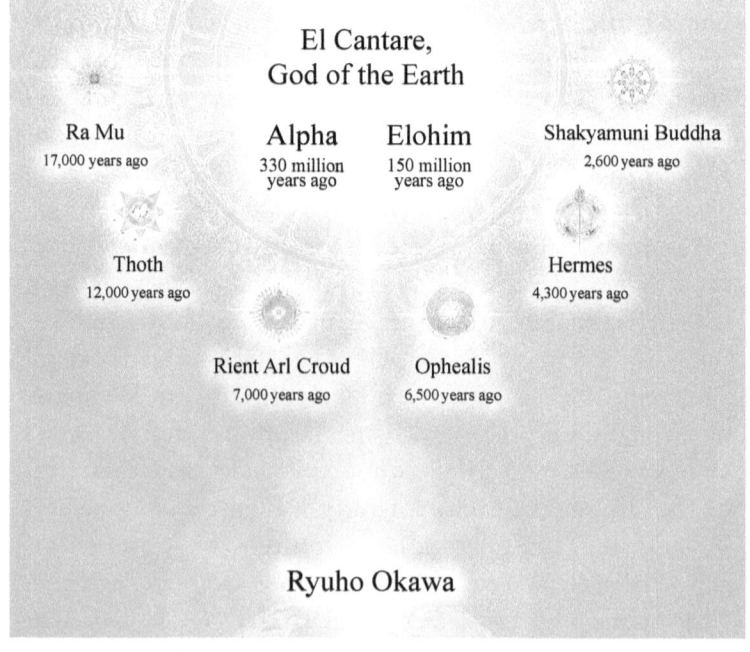

Alpha is a part of the core consciousness of El Cantare who descended to Earth around 330 million years ago. Alpha preached Earth's Truths to harmonize and unify Earth-born humans and space people who came from other planets.

Elohim is a part of El Cantare's core consciousness who descended to Earth around 150 million years ago. He gave wisdom, mainly on the differences of light and darkness, good and evil.

Shakyamuni Buddha was born as a prince into the Shakya Clan in India around 2,600 years ago. When he was 29 years old, he renounced the world and sought enlightenment. He later attained Great Enlightenment and founded Buddhism.

Hermes is one of the 12 Olympian gods in Greek mythology, but the spiritual Truth is that he taught the teachings of love and progress around 4,300 years ago that became the origin of the current Western civilization. He is a hero that truly existed.

Ophealis was born in Greece around 6,500 years ago and was the leader who took an expedition to as far as Egypt. He is the God of miracles, prosperity, and arts, and is known as Osiris in the Egyptian mythology.

Rient Arl Croud was born as a king of the ancient Incan Empire around 7,000 years ago and taught about the mysteries of the mind. In the heavenly world, he is responsible for the interactions that take place between various planets.

Thoth was an almighty leader who built the golden age of the Atlantic civilization around 12,000 years ago. In the Egyptian mythology, he is known as god Thoth.

Ra Mu was a leader who built the golden age of the civilization of Mu around 17,000 years ago. As a religious leader and a politician, he ruled by uniting religion and politics.

WHAT IS A SPIRITUAL MESSAGE?

We are all spiritual beings living on this earth. The following is the mechanism behind Master Ryuho Okawa's spiritual messages.

1 You are a spirit

People are born into this world to gain wisdom through various experiences and return to the other world when their lives end. We are all spirits and repeat this cycle in order to refine our souls.

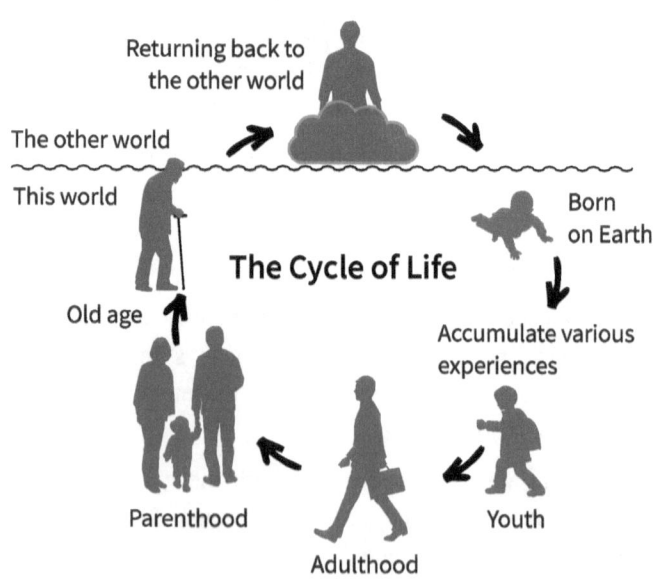

2 You have a guardian spirit

Guardian spirits are those who protect the people who are living on this earth. Each of us has a guardian spirit that watches over us and guides us from the other world. They were us in our past life, and are identical in how we think.

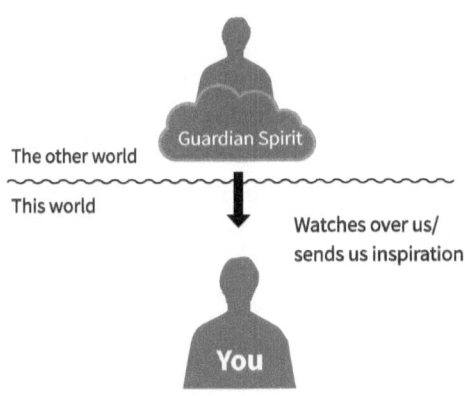

3 How spiritual messages work

Master Ryuho Okawa, through his enlightenment, is capable of summoning any spirit from anywhere in the world, including the spirit world.

Master Okawa's way of receiving spiritual messages is fundamentally different from that of other psychic mediums who undergo trances and are thereby completely taken over by the spirits they are channeling.

Master Okawa's attainment of a high level of enlightenment enables him to retain full control of his consciousness and body throughout the duration of the spiritual message. To allow the spirits to express their own thoughts and personalities freely, however, Master Okawa usually softens the dominancy of his consciousness. This way, he is able to keep his own philosophies out of the way and ensure that the spiritual messages are pure expressions of the spirits he is channeling.

Since guardian spirits think at the same subconscious level as the person living on earth, Master Okawa can summon the spirit and find out what the person on earth is actually thinking. If the person has already returned to the other world, the spirit can give messages to the people living on earth through Master Okawa.

Since 2009, more than 1,200 sessions of spiritual messages have been openly recorded by Master Okawa, and the majority of these have been published. Spiritual messages from the guardian spirits of people living today such as Donald Trump, former Japanese Prime Minister Shinzo Abe and Chinese President Xi Jinping, as well as spiritual messages sent from the spirit world by Jesus Christ, Muhammad, Thomas Edison, Mother Teresa, Steve Jobs and Nelson Mandela are just a tiny pack of spiritual messages that were published so far.

Domestically, in Japan, these spiritual messages are being read by a wide range of politicians and mass media, and the high-level contents of these books are delivering an impact even more on politics, news and public opinion. In recent years, there have been spiritual messages recorded in English, and English translations are being done on the spiritual messages given in Japanese. These have been published overseas, one after another, and have started to shake the world.

For more about spiritual messages and a complete list of books in the Spiritual Interview Series, visit okawabooks.com

ABOUT HAPPY SCIENCE

Happy Science is a global movement that empowers individuals to find purpose and spiritual happiness and to share that happiness with their families, societies, and the world. With more than 12 million members around the world, Happy Science aims to increase awareness of spiritual truths and expand our capacity for love, compassion, and joy so that together we can create the kind of world we all wish to live in.

Activities at Happy Science are based on the Principles of Happiness (Love, Wisdom, Self-Reflection, and Progress). These principles embrace worldwide philosophies and beliefs, transcending boundaries of culture and religions.

Love teaches us to give ourselves freely without expecting anything in return; it encompasses giving, nurturing, and forgiving.

Wisdom leads us to the insights of spiritual truths, and opens us to the true meaning of life and the will of God (the universe, the highest power, Buddha).

Self-Reflection brings a mindful, nonjudgmental lens to our thoughts and actions to help us find our truest selves—the essence of our souls—and deepen our connection to the highest power. It helps us attain a clean and peaceful mind and leads us to the right life path.

Progress emphasizes the positive, dynamic aspects of our spiritual growth—actions we can take to manifest and spread happiness around the world. It's a path that not only expands our soul growth, but also furthers the collective potential of the world we live in.

PROGRAMS AND EVENTS

The doors of Happy Science are open to all. We offer a variety of programs and events, including self-exploration and self-growth programs, spiritual seminars, meditation and contemplation sessions, study groups, and book events.

Our programs are designed to:
* Deepen your understanding of your purpose and meaning in life
* Improve your relationships and increase your capacity to love unconditionally
* Attain peace of mind, decrease anxiety and stress, and feel positive
* Gain deeper insights and a broader perspective on the world
* Learn how to overcome life's challenges
    ... and much more.

For more information, visit happy-science.org.

OUR ACTIVITIES

Happy Science does other various activities to provide support for those in need.

- You Are An Angel! General Incorporated Association

  Happy Science has a volunteer network in Japan that encourages and supports children with disabilities as well as their parents and guardians.

- Never Mind School for Truancy

  At 'Never Mind,' we support students who find it very challenging to attend schools in Japan. We also nurture their self-help spirit and power to rebound against obstacles in life based on Master Okawa's teachings and faith.

- "Prevention Against Suicide" Campaign since 2003

  A nationwide campaign to reduce suicides; over 20,000 people commit suicide every year in Japan. "The Suicide Prevention Website-Words of Truth for You-" presents spiritual prescriptions for worries such as depression, lost love, extramarital affairs, bullying and work-related problems, thereby saving many lives.

- Support for Anti-bullying Campaigns

  Happy Science provides support for a group of parents and guardians, Network to Protect Children from Bullying, a general incorporated foundation launched in Japan to end bullying, including those that can even be called a criminal offense. So far, the network received more than 5,000 cases and resolved 90% of them.

- The Golden Age Scholarship
  This scholarship is granted to students who can contribute greatly and bring a hopeful future to the world.

- Success No.1
  Buddha's Truth Afterschool Academy
  Happy Science has over 180 classrooms throughout Japan and in several cities around the world that focus on afterschool education for children. The education focuses on faith and morals in addition to supporting children's school studies.

- Angel Plan V
  For children under the age of kindergarten, Happy Science holds classes for nurturing healthy, positive, and creative boys and girls.

- Future Stars Training Department
  The Future Stars Training Department was founded within the Happy Science Media Division with the goal of nurturing talented individuals to become successful in the performing arts and entertainment industry.

- NEW STAR PRODUCTION Co., Ltd.
  ARI Production Co., Ltd.
  We have companies to nurture actors and actresses, artists, and vocalists. They are also involved in film production.

ABOUT HAPPINESS REALIZATION PARTY

The Happiness Realization Party (HRP) was founded in May 2009 by Master Ryuho Okawa as part of the Happy Science Group to offer concrete and proactive solutions to the current issues such as military threats from North Korea and China and the long-term economic recession. HRP aims to implement drastic reforms of the Japanese government, thereby bringing peace and prosperity to Japan. To accomplish this, HRP proposes two key policies:

1) Strengthening the national security and the Japan-U.S. alliance, which plays a vital role in the stability of Asia.

2) Improving the Japanese economy by implementing drastic tax cuts, taking monetary easing measures and creating new major industries.

HRP advocates that Japan should offer a model of a religious nation that allows diverse values and beliefs to coexist, and that contributes to global peace.

For more information, visit en.hr-party.jp

HAPPY SCIENCE ACADEMY JUNIOR AND SENIOR HIGH SCHOOL

Happy Science Academy Junior and Senior High School is a boarding school founded with the goal of educating the future leaders of the world who can have a big vision, persevere, and take on new challenges.

Currently, there are two campuses in Japan; the Nasu Main Campus in Tochigi Prefecture, founded in 2010, and the Kansai Campus in Shiga Prefecture, founded in 2013.

Nasu Main Campus

Kansai Campus

 **HAPPY SCIENCE UNIVERSITY**

THE FOUNDING SPIRIT AND THE GOAL OF EDUCATION

Based on the founding philosophy of the university, "Exploration of happiness and the creation of a new civilization," education, research and studies will be provided to help students acquire deep understanding grounded in religious belief and advanced expertise with the objectives of producing "great talents of virtue" who can contribute in a broad-ranging way to serve Japan and the international society.

FACULTIES

Faculty of human happiness

Students in this faculty will pursue liberal arts from various perspectives with a multidisciplinary approach, explore and envision an ideal state of human beings and society.

Faculty of successful management

This faculty aims to realize successful management that helps organizations to create value and wealth for society and to contribute to the happiness and the development of management and employees as well as society as a whole.

Faculty of future creation

Students in this faculty study subjects such as political science, journalism, performing arts and artistic expression, and explore and present new political and cultural models based on truth, goodness and beauty.

Faculty of future industry

This faculty aims to nurture engineers who can resolve various issues facing modern civilization from a technological standpoint and contribute to the creation of new industries of the future.

CONTACT INFORMATION

Happy Science is a worldwide organization with faith centers around the globe. For a comprehensive list of centers, visit the worldwide directory at *happy-science.org*. The following are some of the many Happy Science locations:

UNITED STATES AND CANADA

New York
79 Franklin St., New York, NY 10013
Phone: 212-343-7972
Fax: 212-343-7973
Email: ny@happy-science.org
Website: happyscience-usa.org

New Jersey
725 River Rd, #102B, Edgewater, NJ 07020
Phone: 201-313-0127
Fax: 201-313-0120
Email: nj@happy-science.org
Website: happyscience-usa.org

Florida
5208 8th St., Zephyrhills, FL 33542
Phone: 813-715-0000
Fax: 813-715-0010
Email: florida@happy-science.org
Website: happyscience-usa.org

Atlanta
1874 Piedmont Ave., NE Suite 360-C
Atlanta, GA 30324
Phone: 404-892-7770
Email: atlanta@happy-science.org
Website: happyscience-usa.org

San Francisco
525 Clinton St.
Redwood City, CA 94062
Phone & Fax: 650-363-2777
Email: sf@happy-science.org
Website: happyscience-usa.org

Los Angeles
1590 E. Del Mar Blvd., Pasadena, CA 91106
Phone: 626-395-7775
Fax: 626-395-7776
Email: la@happy-science.org
Website: happyscience-usa.org

Orange County
10231 Slater Ave., #204
Fountain Valley, CA 92708
Phone: 714-659-1501
Email: oc@happy-science.org
Website: happyscience-usa.org

San Diego
7841 Balboa Ave., Suite #202
San Diego, CA 92111
Phone: 626-395-7775
Fax: 626-395-7776
E-mail: sandiego@happy-science.org
Website: happyscience-usa.org

Hawaii
Phone: 808-591-9772
Fax: 808-591-9776
Email: hi@happy-science.org
Website: happyscience-usa.org

Kauai
3343 Kanakolu Street, Suite 5
Lihue, HI 96766, U.S.A.
Phone: 808-822-7007
Fax: 808-822-6007
Email: kauai-hi@happy-science.org
Website: happyscience-usa.org

Toronto
845 The Queensway
Etobicoke ON M8Z 1N6 Canada
Phone: 1-416-901-3747
Email: toronto@happy-science.org
Website: happy-science.ca

Vancouver
#201-2607 East 49th Avenue
Vancouver, BC, V5S 1J9, Canada
Phone: 1-604-437-7735
Fax: 1-604-437-7764
Email: vancouver@happy-science.org
Website: happy-science.ca

INTERNATIONAL

Tokyo
1-6-7 Togoshi, Shinagawa
Tokyo, 142-0041 Japan
Phone: 81-3-6384-5770
Fax: 81-3-6384-5776
Email: tokyo@happy-science.org
Website: happy-science.org

Seoul
74, Sadang-ro 27-gil,
Dongjak-gu, Seoul, Korea
Phone: 82-2-3478-8777
Fax: 82-2-3478-9777
Email: korea@happy-science.org
Website: happyscience-korea.org

London
3 Margaret St.
London,W1W 8RE United Kingdom
Phone: 44-20-7323-9255
Fax: 44-20-7323-9344
Email: eu@happy-science.org
Website: happyscience-uk.org

Taipei
No. 89, Lane 155, Dunhua N. Road
Songshan District, Taipei City 105, Taiwan
Phone: 886-2-2719-9377
Fax: 886-2-2719-5570
Email: taiwan@happy-science.org
Website: happyscience-tw.org

Sydney
516 Pacific Hwy, Lane Cove North,
NSW 2066, Australia
Phone: 61-2-9411-2877
Fax: 61-2-9411-2822
Email: sydney@happy-science.org

Malaysia
No 22A, Block 2, Jalil Link Jalan Jalil
Jaya 2, Bukit Jalil 57000, Kuala Lumpur, Malaysia
Phone: 60-3-8998-7877
Fax: 60-3-8998-7977
Email: malaysia@happy-science.org
Website: happyscience.org.my

Brazil Headquarters
Rua. Domingos de Morais 1154,
Vila Mariana, Sao Paulo SP
CEP 04010-100, Brazil
Phone: 55-11-5088-3800
Email: sp@happy-science.org
Website: happyscience.com.br

Nepal
Kathmandu Metropolitan City Ward
No. 15,
Ring Road, Kimdol,
Sitapaila Kathmandu, Nepal
Phone: 97-714-272931
Email: nepal@happy-science.org

Jundiai
Rua Congo, 447, Jd. Bonfiglioli
Jundiai-CEP, 13207-340
Phone: 55-11-4587-5952
Email: jundiai@happy-science.org

Uganda
Plot 877 Rubaga Road, Kampala
P.O. Box 34130, Kampala, Uganda
Phone: 256-79-4682-121
Email: uganda@happy-science.org
Website: happyscience-uganda.org

ABOUT IRH PRESS

IRH Press Co., Ltd., based in Tokyo, was founded in 1987 as a publishing division of Happy Science. IRH Press publishes religious and spiritual books, journals, magazines and also operates broadcast and film production enterprises. For more information, visit *okawabooks.com*.

Follow us on:
Facebook: Okawa Books
Goodreads: Ryuho Okawa
Pinterest: Okawa Books
Twitter: Okawa Books
Instagram: OkawaBooks

――― **NEWSLETTER** ―――

To receive book related news, promotions and events, please subscribe to our newsletter below.

https://okawabooks.us11.list-manage.com/subscribe?u=1fc70960eefd92668052ab7f8&id=2fbd8150ef

――― **MEDIA** ―――

OKAWA BOOK CLUB

A conversation about Ryuho Okawa's titles, topics ranging from self-help, current affairs, spirituality and religions.

Available at iTunes, Spotify and Amazon Music.

Apple iTunes:
https://podcasts.apple.com/us/podcast/okawa-book-club/id1527893043

Spotify:
https://open.spotify.com/show/09mpgX2iJ6stVm4eBRdo2b

Amazon Music:
https://music.amazon.com/podcasts/7b759f24-ff72-4523-bfee-24f48294998f/Okawa-Book-Club

BOOKS BY RYUHO OKAWA

RYUHO OKAWA'S LAWS SERIES

The Laws Series is an annual volume of books that are mainly comprised of Ryuho Okawa's lectures on various topics that highlight principles and guidelines for the activities of Happy Science every year. *The Laws of the Sun*, the first publication of the laws series, ranked in the annual best-selling list in Japan in 1987. Since then, all of the laws series' titles have ranked in the annual best-selling list for more than two decades, setting socio-cultural trends in Japan and around the world.

The 27th Laws Series
THE LAWS OF SECRET
AWAKEN TO THIS NEW WORLD AND CHANGE YOUR LIFE

Paperback • 248 pages • $16.95
ISBN: 978-1-942125-81-5

Our physical world coexists with the multi-dimensional spirit world and we are constantly interacting with some kind of spiritual energy, whether positive or negative, without consciously realizing it. This book reveals how our lives are affected by invisible influences, including the spiritual reasons behind influenza, the novel coronavirus infection, and other illnesses.

The new view of the world in this book will inspire you to change your life in a better direction, and to become someone who can give hope and courage to others in this age of confusion.

For a complete list of books, visit okawabooks.com

THE TRILOGY

The first three volumes of the Laws Series, *The Laws of the Sun*, *The Golden Laws*, and *The Nine Dimensions* make a trilogy that completes the basic framework of the teachings of God's Truths. *The Laws of the Sun* discusses the structure of God's Laws, *The Golden Laws* expounds on the doctrine of time, and *The Nine Dimensions* reveals the nature of space.

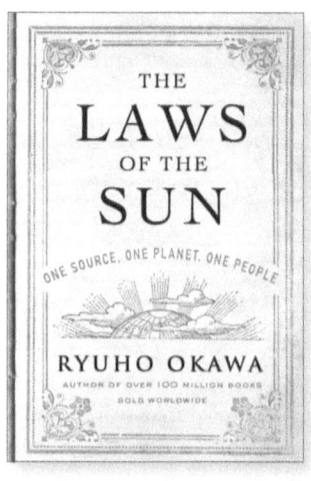

THE LAWS OF THE SUN

ONE SOURCE, ONE PLANET, ONE PEOPLE

Paperback • 288 pages • $15.95
ISBN: 978-1-942125-43-3

IMAGINE IF YOU COULD ASK GOD why He created this world and what spiritual laws He used to shape us—and everything around us. If we could understand His designs and intentions, we could discover what our goals in life should be and whether our actions move us closer to those goals or farther away.

At a young age, a spiritual calling prompted Ryuho Okawa to outline what he innately understood to be universal truths for all humankind. In *The Laws of the Sun*, Okawa outlines these laws of the universe and provides a road map for living one's life with greater purpose and meaning.

In this powerful book, Ryuho Okawa reveals the transcendent nature of consciousness and the secrets of our multidimensional universe and our place in it. By understanding the different stages of love and following the Buddhist Eightfold Path, he believes we can speed up our eternal process of development. *The Laws of the Sun* shows the way to realize true happiness—a happiness that continues from this world through the other.

For a complete list of books, visit okawabooks.com

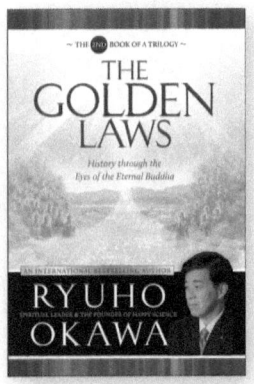

THE GOLDEN LAWS
HISTORY THROUGH THE EYES OF THE ETERNAL BUDDHA

Paperback • 201 pages • $14.95
ISBN: 978-1-941779-81-1

Throughout history, Great Guiding Spirits of Light have been present on Earth in both the East and the West at crucial points in human history to further our spiritual development. *The Golden Laws* reveals how Divine Plan has been unfolding on Earth, and outlines 5,000 years of the secret history of humankind. Once we understand the true course of history, through past, present and into the future, we cannot help but become aware of the significance of our spiritual mission in the present age.

THE NINE DIMENSIONS
UNVEILING THE LAWS OF ETERNITY

Paperback • 168 pages • $15.95
ISBN: 978-0-982698-56-3

This book is a window into the mind of our loving God, who designed this world and the vast, wondrous world of our afterlife as a school with many levels through which our souls learn and grow. When the religions and cultures of the world discover the truth of their common spiritual origin, they will be inspired to accept their differences, come together under faith in God, and build an era of harmony and peaceful progress on Earth.

For a complete list of books, visit okawabooks.com

LAWS SERIES

THE LAWS OF HAPPINESS
LOVE, WISDOM, SELF-REFLECTION AND PROGRESS

Paperback • 264 pages • $16.95
ISBN: 978-1-942125-70-9

This book endeavors to answer the question, "What is true happiness?" This milestone text introduces four distinct principles, based on the "Laws of Mind" and sourced from Okawa's real-world experience, to guide readers towards sustainable happiness. Okawa's four "Principles of Happiness" present an easy, yet profound framework to ground this rapidly advanced and highly competitive society. In practice, Okawa outlines pragmatic steps to revitalize our ambition to lead a happier and meaningful life.

THE LAWS OF GREAT ENLIGHTENMENT
ALWAYS WALK WITH BUDDHA

Paperback • 232 pages • $17.95
ISBN: 978-1-942125-62-4

Constant self-blame for mistakes, setbacks, or failures and feelings of unforgivingness toward others are hard to overcome. Through the power of enlightenment we can learn to forgive ourselves and others, overcome life's problems, and courageously create a brighter future ourselves. *The Laws of Great Enlightenment* addresses the core problems of life that people often struggle with and offers advice on how to overcome them based on spiritual truths.

For a complete list of books, visit okawabooks.com

THE LAWS OF HOPE
THE LIGHT IS HERE

Paperback • 224 pages • $16.95
ISBN: 978-1-942125-76-1

This book provides ways to bring light and hope to ourselves through our own efforts, even in the midst of sufferings and adversities. Inspired by a wish to bring happiness, success, and hope to humanity, Okawa shows us how to look at and think about our lives and circumstances. He says that hopes come true when we have the right mindset inside us.

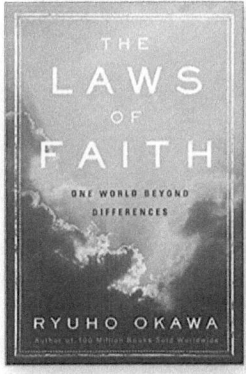

THE LAWS OF FAITH
ONE WORLD BEYOND DIFFERENCES

Paperback • 208 pages • $15.95
ISBN: 978-1-942125-34-1

Ryuho Okawa preaches at the core of a new universal religion from various angles while integrating logical and spiritual viewpoints in mind with current world situations. This book offers us the key to accept diversities beyond differences in ethnicity, religion, race, gender, descent, and so on, harmonize the individuals and nations and create a world filled with peace and prosperity.

For a complete list of books, visit okawabooks.com

MESSAGES FROM SPACE BEINGS

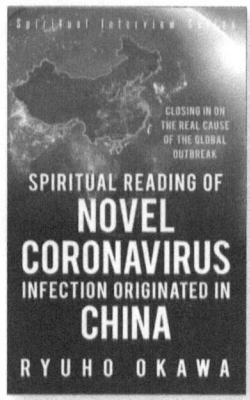

SPIRITUAL READING OF NOVEL CORONAVIRUS INFECTION ORIGINATED IN CHINA

CLOSING IN ON THE REAL CAUSE OF THE GLOBAL OUTBREAK

Paperback • 278 pages • $13.95
ISBN: 978-1-943869-77-0

This worldwide pandemic is not a mere act of nature nor a coincidence, but rather, heaven's warning to humanity, especially China. Through this book, you can find out "the immunity" against the novel coronavirus, among other shocking truths.

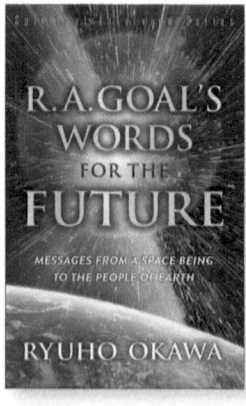

R. A. GOAL'S WORDS FOR THE FUTURE

MESSAGES FROM A SPACE BEING TO THE PEOPLE OF EARTH

Paperback • 174 pages • $11.95
ISBN: 978-1-943928-10-1

R. A. Goal, a certified messiah from Planet Andalucia Beta in Ursa Minor, gives humans on Earth three predictions for 2021. They include the prospect of the novel coronavirus pandemic, the outlook of economic crisis, and the risk of war. But the hope is that Savior is now born on Earth to overcome any bad predictions. Now is the time to open our hearts and listen to the words from R. A. Goal.

For a complete list of books, visit okawabooks.com

THE TRUE HEART OF YAIDRON
GUIDELINES FOR HUMANKIND SUFFERING FROM THE CORONAVIRUS

Paperback • 144 pages • $11.95
ISBN: 978-1-943928-04-0

What are the real cause and evil schemes behind the worldwide coronavirus crisis? Out of compassion, this book reveals truths about the all-out global war now being waged by the evil power in East Asia that's destroying the power of the people. Discover the movement that's trying to bring together the powers of the West, India, and Asia by the belief of "With Savior," to save humankind and create the new golden future of Earth.

WITH SAVIOR
MESSAGES FROM SPACE BEING YAIDRON

Paperback • 232 pages • $13.95
ISBN: 978-1-943869-94-7

The human race is now faced with multiple unprecedented crises. Perhaps God is warning us humans to reconsider our materialistic and arrogant ways. Fortunately, God has sent us a savior, who is now teaching us to repent and showing us the path we should choose. In this book, space being Yaidron sends his warnings and messages of hope.

For a complete list of books, visit okawabooks.com

CONSIDERING THE FUTURE OF THE WORLD

TRUMP SHALL NEVER DIE

HIS DETERMINATION TO COME BACK

Paperback • 206 pages • $11.95
ISBN: 978-1-943928-08-8

This book unveiled Mr. Donald Trump's true thoughts never reported by the media through spiritual interview with the guardian spirit of him. The topics include the "madness" found in GAFA and the mainstream media, Mr. Trump's views on the coronavirus vaccine and global warming, and the true aim of "Make America Great Again."

THE XI JINPING THOUGHT NOW

Paperback • 212 pages • $13.95
ISBN: 978-1-943928-05-7

With the launch of Biden administration in the U.S. and the 100th anniversary of the founding of the Chinese Communist Party approaching, China has been expanding its military threat and reinforcing its influence over the world. What urges China to seek global hegemony? This book unveils the "dark being" behind the Xi Jinping Thought.

For a complete list of books, visit okawabooks.com

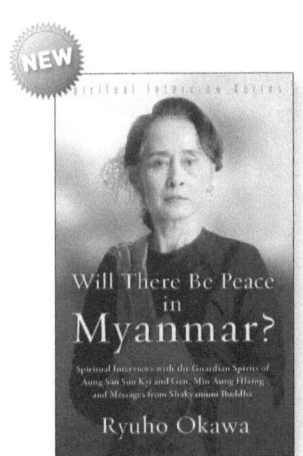

WILL THERE BE PEACE IN MYANMAR?

SPIRITUAL INTERVIEWS WITH THE GUARDIAN SPIRITS OF AUNG SAN SUU KYI AND GEN. MIN AUNG HLAING AND MESSAGES FROM SHAKYAMUNI BUDDHA

Paperback • 194 pages • $11.95
ISBN: 978-1-943928-12-5

February 2021. Tatmadaw, Myanmar Armed Forces, staged a coup against the pro-democracy leader Aung San Suu Kyi. Behind the nation's army lurks one of the world's major powers working to gain its influence on Myanmar. But, now is the time for the world to change. Words from Shakyamuni Buddha will also help bring peace to Myanmar, Asia, and the world.

HOW TO SURVIVE THE CORONAVIRUS RECESSION

Paperback • 171 pages • $14.95
ISBN: 978-1-943869-97-8

From the perspectives of both economics and health, this book delves into how you can survive the coronavirus recession. As taught by the author Ryuho Okawa, there is a strong relationship between your spiritual health and immunity, and he demonstrates the mindset you should have as well as introduces a very effective meditation that you can do to truly strengthen your immunity.

For a complete list of books, visit okawabooks.com

RECOMMENDED SPIRITUAL MESSAGES

JOHN LENNON'S MESSAGE FROM HEAVEN

ON THE SPIRIT OF LOVE AND PEACE, MUSIC, AND THE INCREDIBLE SECRET OF HIS SOUL

Paperback • 310 pages • $13.95
ISBN: 978-1-943869-78-7

John Lennon's Message from Heaven is a compilation of his spiritual message held in three separate parts. He speaks his real thoughts and feelings on many topics regarding the world's current and past conditions, and key aspects of the life he lived on Earth.

SPIRITUAL INTERVIEW WITH BRUCE LEE

THE RESURRECTION OF THE DRAGON

Paperback • 113 pages • $9.95
ISBN: 978-1-943869-34-3

Here, we present you, martial artists and Bruce Lee fans all over the world who respect him even after his death over 40 years ago, the truth revealed by the "Dragon" who is still fighting evil in the Spirit World. He speaks a lot about his own kung fu philosophy that he had deepened further after his death, as well as the truth of his young death and the mission of his soul.

For a complete list of books, visit okawabooks.com

SPIRITUAL INTERVIEW WITH PRINCESS DIANA

HER MESSAGES, 20 YEARS AFTER HER DEATH

Paperback • 103 pages • $9.95
ISBN: 978-1-943869-23-7

This spiritual message tells us about the background of the Paris accident and what Diana has been doing since her death. Diana said that through the spiritual conversation, she was able to deepen her understanding on the Spirit World and her own soul, and that she gained the key to return to the world of goddesses in Heaven.

THE SHAPE OF THINGS IN 2100

H. G. WELLS PREDICTS THE FUTURE OF THE WORLD

Paperback • 176 pages • $14.95
ISBN: 978-1-941779-37-8

What does H. G. Wells see for our future today? What was the nature of the crisis and hope he predicted in his novel, The Shape of Things to Come? His answers to these questions reveal the importance of bringing change to our world today to build a positive future.

For a complete list of books, visit okawabooks.com

BOOKS ON THE TRUTH OF THE SPIRIT WORLD

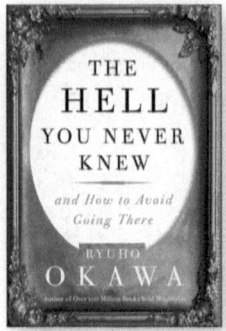

THE HELL YOU NEVER KNEW
AND HOW TO AVOID GOING THERE

Paperback • 192 pages • $15.95
ISBN: 978-1-942125-52-5

From ancient times, people have been warned of the danger of falling to Hell. But does the world of Hell truly exist? If it does, what kind of people would go there? Through his spiritual abilities, Ryuho Okawa found out that Hell is only a small part of the vast Spirit World, yet more than half of the people today go there after they die.

THE REAL EXORCIST
ATTAIN WISDOM TO CONQUER EVIL

Paperback • 208 pages • $16.95
ISBN: 978-1-942125-67-9

This is a profound spiritual text backed by the author's nearly 40 years of real-life experience with spiritual phenomena. In it, Okawa teaches how we may discern and overcome our negative tendencies, by acquiring the right knowledge, mindset and lifestyle.

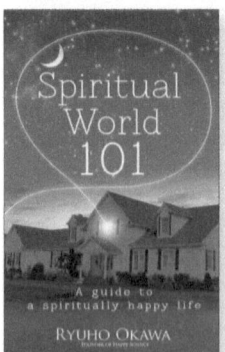

SPIRITUAL WORLD 101
A GUIDE TO A SPIRITUALLY HAPPY LIFE

Paperback • 184 pages • $14.95
ISBN: 978-1-941779-43-9

This book is a spiritual guidebook that will answer all your questions about the spiritual world, with illustrations and diagrams explaining about your guardian spirit and the secrets of God and Buddha. By reading this book, you will be able to understand the true meaning of life and find happiness in everyday life.

For a complete list of books, visit okawabooks.com

THE TRUE EIGHTFOLD PATH

GUIDEPOSTS FOR SELF-INNOVATION

Paperback • 272 pages • $16.95
ISBN: 978-1-942125-80-8

This book explains how we can apply the Eightfold Path, one of the main pillars of Shakyamuni Buddha's teachings, as everyday guideposts in the modern-age to achieve self-innovation to live better and make positive changes in these uncertain times.

THE ESSENCE OF BUDDHA

THE PATH TO ENLIGHTENMENT

Paperback • 208 pages • $14.95
ISBN: 978-1-942125-06-8

In this book, Ryuho Okawa imparts in simple and accessible language his wisdom about the essence of Shakyamuni Buddha's philosophy of life and enlightenment–teachings that have been inspiring people all over the world for over 2,500 years. By offering a new perspective on core Buddhist thoughts, Okawa brings these teachings to life for modern people. This book distills a way of life that anyone can practice to achieve a life of self-growth, compassionate living, and true happiness.

THE MIRACLE OF MEDITATION

OPENING YOUR LIFE TO PEACE, JOY,
AND THE POWER WITHIN

Paperback • 207 pages • $15.95
ISBN: 978-1-942125-09-9

This book introduces various types of meditation, including calming meditation, purposeful meditation, reading meditation, reflective meditation, and meditation to communicate with heaven. Through reading and practicing meditation in this book, we can experience the miracle of meditation, which is to start living a life of peace, happiness, and success.

For a complete list of books, visit okawabooks.com

UFOS CAUGHT ON CAMERA!
A Spiritual Investigation on Videos and Photos
of the Luminous Objects Visiting Earth

THE LAWS OF SUCCESS
A Spiritual Guide to Turning Your Hopes into Reality

THE STARTING POINT OF HAPPINESS
An Inspiring Guide to Positive Living with
Faith, Love, and Courage

WORRY-FREE LIVING
Let Go of Stress and Live in Peace and Happiness

THE STRONG MIND
The Art of Building the Inner Strength
to Overcome Life's Difficulties

INVINCIBLE THINKING
An Essential Guide for a Lifetime of
Growth, Success, and Triumph

THINK BIG!
Be Positive and Be Brave to Achieve Your Dreams

CHANGE YOUR LIFE, CHANGE THE WORLD
A Spiritual Guide to Living Now

INVITATION TO HAPPINESS
7 Inspirations from Your Inner Angel

For a complete list of books, visit okawabooks.com

MUSIC BY RYUHO OKAWA

THE THUNDER

a composition for repelling the Coronavirus

We have been granted this music from our Lord. It will repel away the novel Coronavirus originated in China. Experience this magnificent powerful music.

Search on YouTube

the thunder coronavirus   for a short ad!

THE EXORCISM

prayer music for repelling Lost Spirits

Feel the divine vibrations of this Japanese and Western exorcising symphony to banish all evil possessions you suffer from and to purify your space!

Search on YouTube

the exorcism repelling   for a short ad!

 Listen online
Spotify **iTunes** **Amazon**

CD available at amazon.com, and Happy Science local branches & **shoja** (temples)

WITH SAVIOR

English version

"Come what may, you shall expect your future"

This is the message of hope to the modern people who are living in the midst of the Coronavirus pandemic, natural disasters, economic depression, and other various crises.

Search on YouTube | with savior | for a short ad!

THE WATER REVOLUTION

English and Chinese version

"Power to the People!"

For the truth and happiness of the 1.4 billion people in China who have no freedom. Love, justice, and sacred rage of God are on this melody that will give you courage to fight to bring peace.

Search on YouTube | the water revolution | for a short ad!

CD available at amazon.com, and Happy Science local branches & shoja (temples)

Listen online

Spotify iTunes Amazon

www.ingramcontent.com/pod-product-compliance
Lightning Source LLC
Chambersburg PA
CBHW030153100526
44592CB00009B/250